W9-CPD-921

Bluefishing

THE ART OF MAKING
THINGS HAPPEN

STEVE SIMS

NORTH STAR WAY

New York   London   Toronto   Sydney   New Delhi

NORTH
STAR
WAY

An Imprint of Simon & Schuster, Inc.
1230 Avenue of the Americas
New York, NY 10020

First North Star Way hardcover edition October 2017

NORTH STAR WAY and colophon are trademarks of Simon & Schuster, Inc.

For information about special discounts for bulk purchases, please contact Simon & Schuster Special Sales at 1-866-506-1949 or business@simonandschuster.com.

The North Star Way Speakers Bureau can bring authors to your live event. For more information or to book an event, contact the North Star Way Speakers Bureau at 1-212-698-8888 or visit our website at www.thenorthstarway.com.

Interior design by Bryden Spevak

Manufactured in the United States of America

10 9 8 7 6 5 4 3 2 1

Library of Congress Cataloging-in-Publication Data

Names: Sims, Steve (Entrepreneur), author.
Title: Bluefishing : the art of making things happen / Steve Sims.
Description: New York : North Star Way, 2017.
Identifiers: LCCN 2017021657 (print) | LCCN 2017035971 (ebook) | ISBN 9781501152535 (ebook) | ISBN 9781501152511 (hardback)
Subjects: LCSH: Creative ability in business. | Decision making. | Entrepreneurship. | Bluefish (Firm) | BISAC: BUSINESS & ECONOMICS / Decision-Making & Problem Solving. | BUSINESS & ECONOMICS / Entrepreneurship.
Classification: LCC HD53 (ebook) | LCC HD53 .S5576 2017 (print) | DDC 650.1—dc23
LC record available at https://lccn.loc.gov/2017021657

ISBN 978-1-5011-5251-1
ISBN 978-1-5011-5253-5 (ebook)

I know a lot of amazingly great people, but Clare is the one who has been there all the way, every step of the way, through the ups and downs and everything in between. She has continually inspired me, supported me, and loved me (even when I didn't deserve it). I owe everything to my beautiful wife, Clare, and I will spend the rest of my life saying thank you.

CONTENTS

CONTENTS

CONTENTS

CONTENTS

CONTENTS

INTRODUCTION

I don't have a business card. But if I did, it would simply say "Concierge." That's the job title.

That's not really what I do, but it's easier than introducing myself to people as, "Hi, I'm Steve Sims, Bluefisher." I hear crickets when I say that. Okay, they wonder, what does *that* mean?

The answer is, I get things done. I get things done for my clients that nobody else can do. Things that no one else would even try. Bluefishers can get anything done. I mean *anything*.

Want to walk the red carpet at Fashion Week, even if you're a quiet banker who has never worn Prada in her life? Maybe you'd like to watch Formula 1 in Monaco with royalty, or tee off with a Masters champion. What if you could hang out backstage with your favorite band, or even sing on stage with them? And just think how cool would it be to appear in a walk-on role on your favorite TV show. How about flying an L-39 in an edge of space flight, or going on an expedition to visit the Titanic?

That's not just a random list of dreams. I've made all those things happen for people, and plenty more. (And those are only the ones I can tell you about.) I even turned someone into James Bond for the weekend. It was a total high-octane experience starting in Monte Carlo and ending in Moscow, complete with scantily clad women, a kidnapping by a Special Ops team, and of course, an Aston Martin.

No joke. This is what I do. This is what my company, Bluefish, does for people who are tired of standing still, tired of the status quo, and who want to do something incredible.

I could fill a book with unbelievable stories of events and experiences I've created for my clients. But that's not what this book is about. This book is about something much more important.

It's about the ability to make seemingly out-of-reach things happen for yourself. It's about the mindset. The belief. The practice. *That's* the thing that matters. That skill, that talent, that art is a much bigger deal than the events we pull off for people. Immeasurably so.

I'm talking about something bigger than any bucket list, more enduring than a one-time event, and far more important than any celebrity meeting or wild weekend could possibly be. I'm talking about something that will change you, your life, your business, your relationships—everything.

That's why I'm writing this book.

David Allen wrote a great productivity book, *Getting Things Done*. Millions of people follow his philosophy for managing workload in an overloaded era and being productive with their time. That's terrific. But Bluefishing isn't about that. Bluefishing is about *making things happen*. Not checking things off your daily to-do list.

Do you want people to say *yes* to you, instead of closing the door in your face? Do you want to stop feeling stuck, stop worrying about looking dumb if you try something that doesn't work? Do you want to actually do all the things you've planned or promised? Do you want to know what it's like to celebrate success after success after success?

Do you want to know what it feels like not to be afraid?

We're all pretty much the same deep down, so I'm going to guess that you want what I want and what everyone I know actually wants. You want adventure, excitement, contentment, and fulfillment. You want to take care of your family, impress your clients, and have people think you're pretty damn smart and effective. Maybe you even want to leave the world a little better place than you found it.

What I'm about to give you in this book is advice from someone who can make anything happen for you. I say this humbly. I say this based on experience. I say this because I know how to do it, and I know you want to learn how to do this for yourself. So keep reading.

Here's a fact: Bluefishing has transformed my life and the lives of those who have used it into every shade of prosperity you could imagine. We've experienced extreme success, adventures, and actual, genuine contentment with our lives. All in spades.

Everybody promises you success in ten easy steps. That's bullshit, and you won't hear it here. What I do, and what I'm going to teach you, is actually very basic. I warn you, though, it's not without pitfalls and speed bumps. You can't cower your way through life and hope to succeed; you're going to have to stick your neck out a little. The only way to grow is to try things and learn for yourself what doesn't work before you can find what does work. But you won't be alone, and I'll show you actual techniques that will change the way you look at everything. It's less method and more mindset.

Once you get it, you're going to have this big aha! moment. I wish I could be there to see it on your face, to see the way you shift your stance, grow a tiny bit taller, and stop being afraid. You'll start to see results, so you'll keep practicing, and you'll see more results. You'll try new things and even cooler stuff will happen. When you really tap into Bluefishing, it'll blow your mind.

The good news is, none of the stuff I am going to teach you is rocket science. If it were, I wouldn't be doing it. Where I come from, I had a less than zero chance of getting where I am today. But now I'm married to my soul mate, we have three beautiful kids, I have great buddies, a mancave full of motorcycles, and a job traveling around the world giving people tremendous joy and fulfillment.

How did I get here? More important, how can you?

Are you ready to learn the Bluefishing art of making things happen?

Let's do it.

ONE

KNOCKING DOWN WALLS

I knock down walls. Pure and simple.

I grew up an Irish boy in East London, the son of a brick mason. West End was posh, East End was by the docks. East End got bombed badly during the war and it had depressing estate houses (you probably call them tenements) all jammed on top of each other. You couldn't walk around the block without seeing someone falling down drunk. It was rough. More than rough. If you don't believe me, try pickled eel. I used to eat them right out of the Thames.

I was a bricklayer with my dad. I hated bricklaying. It is one of the absolute hardest of all the construction trades. My father and nearly every man in my family did it, so of course they expected that I would too. I was a big guy even at an early age, so I had to carry the hod, a bloody big three-sided box for carrying a bunch of bricks around. It weighed about eighty pounds. The hod of bricks had to be hoisted on your shoulder while you climbed straight up the ladder. One mason needed at least one thousand bricks a day. That meant hard work, no slacking allowed, no whining. It was, literally, back-breaking work.

I did this job all through my teens and I despised every day of it. My teenage self would clobber me now for what I'm about to say, but looking back (and now that I'm dry and warm and not covered in bruises and bits of cement) I have to admit that I'm glad this was my start in life. I learned a rock-solid work ethic, which is a key advantage in business and life and everything in between. Knowing hard manual labor gave me an edge, too. When you're working in an office lifting up a phone or typing emails, I don't care who the hell you are, that's not hard work. Yes, there's an art to negotiation, and brain work is tough. But when it's five o'clock in the morning and it's pissing down rain and you're starting to crank up a cement mixer, that's hard work, okay? It gave me something that many people don't have.

Believe me, back when I was actually doing it, I wanted nothing more than to get out. Not just because it was grueling work, but also because there was something wrong with the path others had chosen for my life.

THAT'S FOR OTHER PEOPLE

The worst part was that there was no getting out of there. There was no doing better, not for the folks from East End. That's not the way people thought in my neighborhood. If you wanted something nice, if you wanted to dream big, you were told, "That's how the other half lives, not us."

One time, my mom and I had to pass through Bond Street, the fancy and famously expensive shopping district across town in West End. My mom secretly loved to window shop as we walked by the posh stores. I could tell one day that she was trying to sneak a peek at a Gucci purse that was displayed under a glittering white light in the window. I said we should go look at it for her, and would you believe she refused to cross the street and look in the window.

"I could never afford those bags," she said in a stiff voice, "there's no point looking."

"Why?" I asked, fearing the answer. I think I was about thirteen at the time.

"Steve, you know, we . . . Well, that's for other people." She put her head down and hurried away from the shop, conversation over.

I wanted to scream. In my head I was yelling "Why!

Why not? Why won't you walk into that shop and take a look? Why can't I do that? What is stopping us?"

I had a family that said, "No, no, no, that's not us. We're this end of town, those people live at that end of town." So, they hunkered down and did their work and never looked up. And that was that.

We all put up so many walls around us. I don't just mean the brick ones my dad and I built back in the day.

That day was my first epiphany. It was the first time I realized that life didn't have to be that way. The first time I saw clearly that there was a different way to think. I remember being shocked to realize that most of the time, what holds us back is entirely in our heads.

YOU DON'T DROWN FROM FALLING IN WATER, YOU DROWN FROM STAYING THERE

I vividly remember the day—no, the *second*—that I knew I was done. It's like a scene from a film frozen in time. I was nineteen years old and pretty beaten down about my lot in life. On that particular day, I had just carried my thirtieth hod up the ladder for the morning. I was at the top of the ladder and I looked down to see who was below me. No reason, just a glance. What I saw, in one suddenly clear moment, was my entire family tree. My dad, uncles, and cousins all down the line of ladders. That image, all of them straight down the line, burned itself into my mind. That was my future. They were me if I didn't get out.

I quit that night. My dad wasn't happy about it, but he understood. He's the one who always told me, "No one drowned from falling in the water. They drowned from staying there." He had taught me to move on when something wasn't working, and that's what I did.

So, by morning, I was out of a job and had to find a new way to make ends meet, but already I was breathing easier. I had nothing to lose and craved adventure. Luckily, I was afraid of boredom, not hard work, and by the end of the first week I had three jobs. I delivered cakes early in the morning, sold insurance in the afternoon, and worked the door at clubs at night. I was working more hours than I ever did in construction, but I was so hungry for new experiences that I didn't care. Besides, *everything* compared to construction is a piece of cake.

The most important thing I noticed in those first weeks was a wall starting to come down inside me. When I moved away from something that wasn't authentically me, I started to feel excited about my days. I felt fear and tightness go away, replaced by the thrill of new ideas and opportunity. I knew I wasn't going to deliver cakes or sell insurance for the rest of my life. It's not like I had suddenly found my calling. What I had found was far bigger. It was the realization that I could do anything.

Of course, it took many more years for that wall, and all my others, to come all the way down. One big leap can make a world of difference, but it still won't change everything overnight. Busting down internal walls takes a lot of practice, even for someone who didn't grow up in East End.

KNOCK 'EM DOWN

It's not just me and my upbringing. We are all constantly taught that we can't do this or that. The average toddler is told "no" more than four hundred times a day. It has been instilled in us for so long, and from such a young age. Stay with the pack. Safety in numbers. Don't wander off. Don't climb too high, swim out too far, ride too fast. Even worse is this one: Don't look dumb. It's made known to every kid, without anyone ever explicitly saying it that, okay, you can ask a question once, that's fine. Maybe twice. But if you still don't get it, you better just nod and pretend you do. Don't risk looking stupid. Ever.

There's a gentleman in London, Suli Breaks, who coined the best phrase I've ever heard. He said "I hate schools, but I love education." My experience in school was that I was shoehorned in to work for someone else and to follow someone else's set of rules. Points were deducted if I ever colored outside the box. If I was told to do something with a couple of people in a team scenario, but I didn't have a relationship with those kids, I was deducted points. The school system tried to teach me that I had to follow and not inspire. We're constantly taught as we get older, "Don't do that. This is right, that's wrong. This is for you, that's not." There is this word, *embarrassment*. You know it. It steers so many people. Chances are that it drives you sometimes, too.

Nine times out of ten, people look at other successful people or watch something on television and think, "That could never be me." So many of us wind up believing this. It cuts us off from everything we ever dreamed of doing.

Have you ever had an idea, a vision for what you wanted to do or make or be? Actor, entrepreneur, restaurant owner, pilot, something that felt right to you, deep in your bones? But then fear paralyzed you and you did nothing bigger or better than the status quo.

Or maybe you actually did it, you got started, and at first people said "Oh, she's so brave," and cheered you on. But then when the going got rough and you entered the long slog of learning to get good, they started to say, "Hey, don't beat yourself up. You tried really hard. Why don't you just give up and get something with a regular pay-check for now?"

Well, you know what I say? I say I was a tenement kid, a bricklayer's son, born to build walls. And now I knock 'em down. If I can do it, anyone can. You can.

I also say it's almost time for me to teach you about Bluefishing. But, first, I have to tell you about the pass-word.

SECRETS FROM
THE BLUEFISHING PLAYBOOK

★ Throw away the thought "That could never be me," and ask, "Why couldn't it?"

★ No one ever drowned from falling in the water . . . they drowned from staying there. Don't be afraid to jump, Bluefisher.

TWO

POWER OF THE PASSWORD

It all started with some bad luck. A few years after I stopped bricklaying, I talked my way into a job at a bank. It was a "real" job and I was totally unqualified for it, but I left London for it anyway. I landed in Hong Kong on a Saturday, I started on Monday, and I was fired on Tuesday. The shortest career of all time.

So, there I was stranded in Hong Kong with no money and no job. I couldn't even afford to fly back home to London. I was out of options and my future was such a blank slate that I was open to the possibility of whatever— you know, the universal whatever—the kind that changes things, but only if you're open to it.

I had worked the door at the club scene back in London, so I picked up a job doing that for some quick cash. Every single bar on my block in Hong Kong was called

Neptune's. Neptune's 1, Neptune's 2, Neptune's 3. They were all about the same inside too, just bar after bar after bar. Not a lot of imagination.

NOT TONIGHT

I worked at Neptune's 1 for no reason other than it was the first one I walked by, and the owner needed a big guy on the door. When the night got going, people would come up to me and say, "Hi, can I go in?" And I'd let them in.

One night a group came up to me and instead of letting them in, I turned them away, saying, "Not tonight, fellas." They looked at me like I had three heads. They thought that I was a guy looking for a fight.

"Look," I said, "It's not because there's anything wrong with you. But it's dead quiet in there, and if you go in, you're gonna feel like you got ripped off."

They had to pay a pretty steep cover charge to get in, and I knew it wasn't worth it.

"Trust me," I continued. "Tonight is really not kicking off in here. But if you walk down the road a bit, that other place is really great tonight. Talk to Billy, tell him Sims sent you down."

Of course, thirty seconds after they left, the owner

scurried over to me and asked why I just sent paying customers away.

"Because they will never come back," I explained. "Not if they have a bad time in there tonight."

To my surprise, instead of firing me, the owner said: "Well, what would you do to kick it up a notch and make it a good time?"

ONE FISH, TWO FISH, RED FISH . . .

So, I started planning a night. A big night. For starters, I got a better DJ and I made sure the prettier bartenders were on duty. This was nothing much, but it was better than the other cookie cutter bars.

The real trick was how I got the word out. Because I had sent them away on previous nights, people would often walk past me and ask, "Hey, Sims, tonight?"

So, this time I said, "Tomorrow's the night. It's happening here. Tell your boys."

And I gave them a password.

People told their friends. They whispered the password to each other. Then they arrived, laughing, and used the password to get in. Passersby could hear the noise and good times coming from inside the bar and asked to go in, but without the password they were out of luck. They got turned away in droves. Meanwhile, the insiders had an amazing night. Everyone wanted to know how they could get the password for the next party. Just like that, I was in business.

At first, this was all just word of mouth. There was no organized invite list or special promotion for the parties. Then I started getting ideas and started putting a structure to it. I would go through the newspapers, and when so-and-so was getting a new job, or so-and-so was celebrating something, I would send a little note. "Hey, Richard, congratulations on your new job. It looks like you're new in town, so I wanted to let you know I'm throwing a party next Thursday night. Call me if you want to know where it's going to be."

When he called, and he always called, I'd say, "This is the location, this is the time, this is the password."

I thought the password was a cool touch, because I figured you had to have a sense of humor to turn up at a club and say something silly to a big guy at the door. I had people walking up to me saying, "Tinky Winky Poe," in order to get in. It was also a great conversation starter for guests. They'd always start out talking about how funny the password was. We came up with all sorts of great ones.

One of my favorites was simply: "One Fish, Two Fish, Red Fish . . ." And that's how we came up with Bluefish.

(Thank you, Dr. Seuss.) I didn't even know it at the time that I was building the foundation and the philosophy of what was going to become the Bluefish business.

After our first few parties really took off, my friends and I started to try out all kinds of new stuff. We started doing promotions, like bringing in a cooler of some new beer that a company was trying to introduce, or sharing exclusive listings for yachts and penthouses with our group of partygoers: whatever we could hustle that gave them something extra that they couldn't get anywhere else.

After about a year of throwing parties that just kept getting bigger and better (and made more and more money), I got invited to Bangkok. I started doing the whole thing all over again. I started finding little bars and clubs and setting up nights, just trying to get different people together. I gave out passwords and started growing a network just like in Hong Kong. It was almost as natural to me as breathing or walking.

BUILDING THE WORLD'S MOST EXCLUSIVE VIP LIST WITHOUT EVEN KNOWING IT

Between Hong Kong and Bangkok, I was starting to earn some serious cash. Without knowing it, I'd already started doing the very early stages of what would become Bluefish. Back then I just looked at it as a way to earn some money and get rich people in my Rolodex. I honestly thought that if I partied with enough rich people, a bank somewhere would offer me a job (because I could recruit these clients, right?), and then I'd be a real success. I laugh now to think of it.

People started asking me how I did what I did. They wanted to analyze it and study it, but that's not my style. I avoid paralysis by analysis at all costs. I will get up and do something and fail at it over and over until I find out how to do it properly, while the analytics group is still trying to work out the demographics, plan the SEO, split test the best time to do something. While they are planning the thing to an early death, I've already tried three or four ways to see if it has any legs.

I did what I did by keeping it raw. We knew what turned people on. People don't want what they can afford. They want what they can't get. They want the mystical, the fantastical. They want excitement; they want adrenaline. These are things you can't get at your neighborhood Walgreens.

A PASSWORD FOR EVERY DOOR

The password opened up doors. So many more than just the one. It made people feel special. They felt like something out of the ordinary was going to happen to them. The password was the key to mystery, excitement, exclusivity. It put desire in the mix.

Once I started to understand what people wanted, what they really wanted, what made their eyes light up, whether they knew it or not, it was easy for me to start making even bigger things happen for them.

All of sudden people started saying, "Sims, I love your parties, can you get me into this concert, can you get me into the Monte Carlo Grand Prix, can you get me backstage at the Cannes Film Festival?" And I'd say, no problem, I'll get you in. Then I'd go home in a panic and try to figure out where Monte Carlo and Cannes even were. I just had this crazy flare for being able to pull shit off. While everyone else would say, "No, it's impossible!" I'd just knock down the front door and say "Can I come in?"

It wasn't long before I had an aha moment of my own. Here I was pulling off lifetime dreams for other people, while I still was just a guy at the door of a club. One day, I actually started to listen to all the things I was saying to other people about getting things done, about how nothing's impossible. Was I a world-class idiot that I hadn't done this for myself? That's when I realized it. Anything I wasn't achieving in life, any doors that were closed to me, I could figure out the password for.

If knocking down walls is about courage and never taking *no* for an answer, unlocking doors is about listening and getting someone to say yes. It is about understanding what someone wants and finding the right key for each door.

That's what Bluefishing can do for you. Bluefishing isn't just for getting into a fancy club. It's for getting where you want to go in business. It's for life.

SECRETS FROM
THE BLUEFISHING PLAYBOOK

★ Avoid analysis by paralysis. While other people are planning things to an early death, Bluefishers have already tried something four different ways and learned what works.

★ There's a password for every door. You just have to listen for it.

THREE

SOMETHING FOR EVERYONE

Herb Cohen coined the phrase "win-win" in 1963 after remembering what his parents told him: "If you treat people nice, they will treat you nice."

I don't know about that as a rule, but the spirit of their advice is right. The idea is simple. There has to be something in it for everyone. You've heard this before and you already generally know how this works. If you're selfish and one-sided and don't consider the other person's point of view, then your fundraising pitch or sales call or third date is going to go nowhere, fast. Win-win is when you make it clear that there's something good in it for everyone involved. *Don't underestimate the power of simplicity.* Don't be easy to understand, be impossible to *mis*understand.

But doing that Bluefish style is operating at a whole

new level. It raises the bar and gets so much more done than you ever thought possible.

I'll give you an example. You can tell me if I'm right or wrong.

ANY WAY YOU WANT IT

A client of mine, a CNBC commentator, wanted to meet the members of Journey. You know, "Don't Stop Believing" and "Wheel in the Sky" and "Any Way You Want It." Yeah. Top ten rock band of all time, Journey.

Dan had earned his way through college many years before as a singer and guitarist in a cover band doing only Journey songs. His cover band did their best to act and look like the originals, which got them more gigs. He spent his college years sleeping on friends' couches, while singing his heart out in local bars for a few bucks. It wasn't a cakewalk, but performing Journey songs got him his degree, which ultimately enabled his future success in media.

Dan was in his midfifties when he called me up. He was working for CNBC, and of course, no longer living on the couch or singing in dive bars. Life was good, so he wanted to go back to Journey, to the actual guys themselves, and say thanks. He wanted to simply say, "You helped drive me in my down days. Your music was what got me going to be able to do the work I needed to do."

That was the entirety of his challenge to me. He just wanted to meet them. When Dan was telling me his story, he came alive just talking about Journey. He threw song titles at me as though they were Bible verses. His passion and gratitude for the band was something you could feel.

So, I said to him quite bluntly, "Let me be completely clear. You're telling me that if you meet these guys, walk up and shake their hands, and then walk away three minutes later, that's enough for you? That's what you want me to arrange for you?" He looked uncertain. He hadn't thought there could be more.

Then we set about really brainstorming on it. "What if we see them at a recording studio and you get to watch them jamming? Or maybe visit during a sound check or something? Something that gives you a bit more of a personal one-on-one interaction, more than just having them sign a book or an album for you or something like that." He said "Absolutely. No question."

From there we took it as far as we could. I got him everything he never imagined. I put him on stage with the band in San Diego. Dan sang four songs as the shortest-term lead singer of Journey. For those four songs, he was in. He was living his dream. We also raised more than six figures for a good cause, which I'll tell you about in a second.

Now, the first thing anyone reading this is going to say, "Well, I can't pay money like that for a dream. That's how the other half lives, but not me."

No. I remember that the original budget was fairly low. Dan made good money with CNBC, but he remembered his days of having nothing at all, and he wasn't the sort of guy to be frivolous.

We started at the end and worked backward. We knew what the dream had to conclude with. We knew that if he was the lead singer of a cover band when he was a kid, the only way to make it really magical would be to have the full band behind him. A meet and greet wasn't the dream; being part of the group was. So we just had to find a way to make it work. We started researching. The way Bluefishers do research is to look for connections. We look for what people are passionate about and look for a way to find a win-win for their passions.

We knew that Dan's nephew had autism. It didn't take too much research to discover that Journey's drummer son also had autism. Both Dan and the drummer had a deep passion for helping autistic kids, thus we were able to use this connection between two people to get them interested in doing something together for the cause. What we did was raise a major chunk of money in the form of charitable donations for Autism Speaks. So we managed to find a route to get what a client wanted, that also benefited someone else. Actually, we benefited a lot of someones, because we wound up creating a major amount of awareness for Autism Speaks. To make that happen we never took our eye off the ball: Our end goal was still to get Dan on stage singing with Journey. We just changed how we got there.

IT'S NOT GOING TO HAPPEN IF IT BENEFITS ONLY YOU

Here's another example of win-win, Bluefish style.

People want to know that you are thinking of them. If you're running a partnership with another business, they want to know you're going to make them look good. If you're on the road away from your family, they want to feel loved even from afar. It doesn't matter if it's business or family or life, if you have any kind of relationship with someone, they want to know that you have them in mind.

I was in an amazing hotel in Italy. I ordered room service and, with it, they dropped off the bar's cocktail menu.

On the back of the cocktail menu, it showed how to make one of their signature cocktails. I loved that.

I went down to reception, carrying the cocktail menu. I said, "I had this in my room and I really like it. I'd like to take a few home with me."

"Certainly," the guy said, "How many would you like?"

I said, "Five hundred."

Well, you can imagine, the first answer was, "Oh, no sir! We don't have that many."

Very politely, I asked, "Can I speak to the manager, or the head of the desk? Can I speak to them for just a second, please?"

The manager came over and here's what I said.

"All right, I was so impressed with this menu and this drink recipe, and I want to send one to each of my top five hundred clients worldwide, and it's got your hotel written all over it. I'm doing all the shipping and mailing, you don't have to do a thing. What would it take to make this happen?"

If you can walk in there giving them a reason to do what you want because it benefits them as much as it benefits you, it's a win-win. Instead of this guy feeling like he was being asked to do a crazy favor for a guest, instead he felt like a genius because he was being given free advertising to five hundred power players.

If you go in with a clear win-win and confidence that

it's going to happen, you'd be surprised how many times you're right. If you go in there with the idea that it's going to fail, or that you're asking too much, or you're giving something the person doesn't really want, you might as well not even go. You've gotta go in there knowing that this is going to happen, but understanding that it's *not* going to happen if it benefits only you.

SHOW THEM THAT YOU'RE DIFFERENT FROM EVERY OTHER PERSON

In this case, I got the menus and the envelopes. Later, when I was on the plane home, with five hours of down-time between New York and Los Angeles, I pulled out my stack of envelopes.

I got my Sharpie out and I wrote, "Hey, Jordan, I know you like a cold drink, found this one in Italy and thought of you. All the best, Steve." Fold it up, stick it in the envelope, stick on stamps, and post it.

For the people out there who have clients, friends, vendors, business partners, it's the same mentality. Show them that you're different from every other person who does business with them. Show them you're a real person, not just a voice on the other end of a phone call, or just another email in their inbox.

LIFE IS A BOX OF CHOCOLATES,
AFTER ALL

My printer is a wonderful woman, and every now and then when I pick up my printouts and booklets and things, I take her a box of chocolates.

I write something like, "Thanks for getting these done so fast, brilliant job." And give it to the woman who processed the order. Don't give it to the manager, don't give it to the delivery boy. Give it to the person who actually did the work for you.

A few times I've called her with a tight turnaround. "Hey, I need to get some cards printed up. I've been given this opportunity and I really want to make it great. But I only have forty-eight hours. What's the turnaround? You think that's possible?"

You'd be amazed by how many times she has said, "We'll push you to the front, don't worry, Steve."

And it gets done.

Win-win doesn't have to operate in the same currencies. Cocktail menus are not the same thing as a powerhouse promotion to five hundred of the world's VIPs. One million dollars to charity is a different unit of currency from one individual's joy at singing on stage with Journey. A box of candy is not the same as my peace of mind knowing I can get something done fast. The point is not eye for an eye or quid pro quo.

The point is to find what the other person is excited about, listen to what matters to them, and show them how helping you benefits them. That's getting it done, Bluefish style.

SECRETS FROM
THE BLUEFISHING PLAYBOOK

★ Don't underestimate the power of simplicity. Don't be easy to understand, be impossible to misunderstand.

★ Nothing's ever going to happen if it benefits only you. Work for win-win, every time.

FOUR

BE THE REAL DEAL

I created and run a high-end concierge service for high net-worth clients. That's what I do. Put that way, though, it sounds like a resume from LinkedIn, doesn't it?

Let's try it another way. I'm the person who makes the magic happen.

People come to me and say, literally, "I want to go to the moon." And I make it happen. Simple as that.

I'm not sure how I got into this, really. I can trace it back to when it started in Hong Kong, but I think it was just one of those things that found me, and I happened to be the guy who's good at getting it done.

A client introduced me once this way, "This is Steve Sims—he gets shit done." It stuck. I am the one guy who gets it done.

GUARANTEE YOU'RE THE REAL DEAL

In Bluefishing, as in actual fishing, the bait catches the fish.

A client of mine had planned a trip to Florence and he wanted to make the visit extra special. He said he wanted to get into some of the galleries, the private art events that are very hard to get into. Or, he said, he'd like to get into the roped-off restoration area of the Palazzo de Vecchio. These things were no-brainers for me, and when I got talking to the guy, I found out he had an ample budget I could work with, so I thought that we could do something even more spectacular for him.

He wound up getting to have a private white table-cloth dinner for six at the foot of Michelangelo's *David*. We closed off the entire Accademia museum just for him. And what's more, halfway through dinner, I had Andrea Bocelli come in and serenade the group.

Now, I've been doing this for twenty years, and I don't take no for an answer. I have the reputation that while I am certainly no Abercrombie model, I sure as hell get it done.

Here's how I got Andrea Bocelli. I phoned his management, which is very easy to do. If you spend five minutes on the Internet, you can find anyone's management or agent. So I contacted the agency. I said that I wanted Andrea Bocelli to come and sing. Bear in mind this was Monday morning, and I wanted him to perform Wednesday evening. I was giving them two days. His agent literally laughed at me on the phone. She said, "We'll get back to you, but don't hold your breath," and hung up on me.

Just the week before, I was in Rome working on getting a client married at the Vatican. So I thought, "In Italy, if I don't have the credibility for something, who do I know who does? Who with real credibility can make that phone call to Andrea's agent to tell her I'm real? I contacted my new pals at the Vatican. I said, "Do you know anyone in Andrea's camp?" They said they did. They made a call. I got a call back asking if I wanted nine or nine-thirty on Wednesday night.

Sometimes, the path to getting it done is knowing people who will guarantee that you're the real deal. That's basically a good advertisement for everyone. I never want to leave any kind of meeting, phone call, presentation, podcast, I never want to leave anything where I'm with another person without it being a win-win. Even when

I went to Bocelli's people, yes, they were making money from the deal, but I knew they had a foundation, so I also made a gesture that was more than monetary, "I'd like to help you with your foundation. I know a lot of people who may be interested in getting involved." I always want to make sure that every environment is a win for everyone involved.

THE EXPERIENCE BEATS THE CASH, EVERY TIME

When I was working on that Vatican event, there was a hotelier in Rome who was doing a lot of work to help me out. He kept certain restaurants open for me. He was going beyond what was necessary for him as the head of a hotel. I found out that he was a massive fan of Maroon 5. I contacted some people I knew in Hollywood. I got a guitar signed by Maroon 5 sent to him.

It didn't cost me a lot of money, but I did pay, and I made a small donation to Maroon 5's charity. They were happy; that concluded the transaction on their end.

On the hotelier's end, he was already getting paid because we were taking over half the hotel, but now he has this guitar. Every time he goes home, there's that signed guitar on the wall. The return on that—he won't forget that. He would have forgotten a pile of extra cash in his pocket. He would have paid the kids' school fees for a month, paid the mortgage for the month, and then the following month he'd just be back to normal, thinking, "Time to pay those bills again" and you're done, you're out of his head. But not with the guitar. The return on investment on any experience given to someone is so much greater than cash.

ALWAYS SWEAT THE SMALL STUFF

How I get all this done for people is quite scientific and it's something I've spent two decades on, but I will try to share it with you. How do I make clients happy? I ask them about their passions. I do a little detective work. I go to Facebook. I find out that they like Maroon 5. I knew one of the receptionists who worked for the hotelier and said, "I was just looking at the boss's Facebook the other day and saw he likes Maroon 5." She confirmed, "Oh yeah, he loves Maroon 5!" Bingo, that's all it takes.

When a prospective client sends me an email about something they want to do, I never answer their email, not really. I write back a quick line and say, "Thank you for reaching out. When is a good time to talk?" It has to be on the phone. I don't know anything about them since they've only written me an email. I need to know them. In order for me to be the real deal, I need to get to the core of what they're really about, too.

ASK WHY THREE TIMES

Once I get them on the phone, I run a bunch of questions by them. "What do you need to get out of this event that's really going to make you cheer? What's got to happen to make you so excited that you lose sleep leading up to it, and so you can't stop talking about it for years to come? Why do you want this?"

Here's the funny thing. When I ask someone to tell me what his or her wildest dream is, they dilute it. Ten times out of ten, people sell themselves short. Remember my client who wanted to meet Journey? That was his goal, just to meet them for a few minutes. I knew we could dream bigger.

What started as an idea to meet them at a concert turned into getting Dan on stage with them to sing a bunch of songs. If we'd acted on his first email without challenging him to dream big and define what he wanted, he'd have just gotten a backstage pass, and that would've been it. He would have gone backstage, stood in line, done a handshake, gotten a selfie, and they wouldn't know anything about him at all. He'd have a little picture to flash around on Facebook and that would be it.

That's why you've got to talk with people. When someone sends you a pitch or a job application or a client request, talk to them. Better yet, ask why. Why do they want to work with you? Why do they want this experience? Why are they selling the thing they're pitching? Don't ask why once. Don't ask twice. Ask why three times. Why do they want the thing they say they want? Then let them answer and ask again: Okay, why that? They answer again, and you go even deeper: Okay, why *that*?

The first why is what they *think* they think, the second why is what they think you want to hear, the third why is what they *feel*.

When you're reaching out to someone for something you need to get done, the same rule applies. Ask them what gets them excited. Find out what a big win would look like for them. Drill down and ask why. If you can't get inside their head and discover their passion—if you can't get inside your own head and find your *own* passion—then you're not Bluefishing.

SECRETS FROM
THE BLUEFISHING PLAYBOOK

★ Ask why at least three times: The first why is what they think they think, the second why is what they think you want to hear, the third why is what they feel.

★ The experience beats the cash, every time. Cash gets spent and forgotten. An experience you can give to someone sticks forever.

FIVE

NO PASSION, NO POINT!

I've always said that passion is my drug of choice. I can get anywhere with passion. I can get further with passion than I can with any amount of money in the world. Passion is my secret weapon.

If I need something from someone, I call them and say, "How much do I have to pay to get you to do this?" they'll hang up faster than you can blink. People don't want to be sold. They also don't want to be bought.

But if I call them and say, "Hey, I have this amazing client who wakes up in the middle of the night dreaming about this thing, and I literally want to make his dream come true. What has to happen for you to help me make that happen for them?" People want to be part of that passion. They want to be part of that fulfillment. Excitement is like electricity.

This is an absolute cornerstone of the Bluefishing technique: passion. If there's no passion, there's no point.

I'm sure there are plenty of people out there thinking, "Passion's great and all, but I have to pay the bills." Okay, I get that. I've been there, too. We all have to pay the bills. And sometimes, if you take a risk that doesn't work out, or if you're in a slump or have a bit of bad luck, or if you just haven't made your break yet, paying the bills can be tough to do.

But if that's all you ever want to do—you just want to pay the bills and get on with it—then this book isn't for you. I didn't write this book to help you stand still and learn to scrape by.

Nope. This is a "get up, get out and make it happen" book. This book is for those of us who have a passion for something deep in our guts and just need some help breaking down walls and learning a few tricks for making things happen. I'm willing to bet that sounds an awful lot like you.

WHAT MAKES THE LIGHTS TURN ON?

Sometimes passion isn't easy to find. I get that, too.

More often than not, people ask me, "How do I even

find my passion? I don't know what I'm passionate about!"

I had one kid at a lecture say to me, "I just got out of college and I don't know what the hell to do. I studied philosophy and I am not getting any jobs. I need to do something for money even though philosophy is my passion. What's my money-making passion? What do I do? How do I find it? I don't know! Help!"

Passion is something that you have to discover. Relax. It takes time. That's normal. Very few people start out knowing at age fifteen or twenty-eight, or even age fifty-five, what their passion is. Finding deep and lasting passion for something is a treasure hunt. It takes time to go on that journey and have those experiences. But once you do, there's real fortune at the end once you discover it. And it's never too late.

I have a friend in Miami whose father was a famous lawyer. Now, my friend is one, too. Simple as that. The problem is, he never wanted to be one and he only did it because his father wanted him to take over the firm. So, my friend has been at it for twenty years or so, hating his work every single day. That makes me so sad. I don't think we really think about wasting our years until we're in our forties or fifties, and we look back and think, "Shit, I spent all that time doing that, and it was something I never even really wanted to do."

Those of us who practice Bluefishing believe that there's no reason to live your life like that. None at all.

THE WORLD IS ENDING

Truthfully, I don't know what river you have to pan to find your passion. I can't tell you what fuel you need in your engine to really move you.

My hope is that you'll take some comfort in hearing that it's not easy, and that most of us have no idea what our biggest and greatest passions even are. My hope is also that you'll be inspired by learning that once you do connect with the thing that drives you and you apply it, it's going to blow your mind.

If you only have twenty minutes left in the day and you can do *anything*, what do you want to do?

What would you do if the world were ending? If you knew that the Earth was going to collide with Mars tomorrow, what would you do right now?

Maybe you're not sure what you're passionate about. Or passionate about most. How do you discover it? I'll tell you. It's crazy. Here it comes.

Be open. Throw open your windows and doors. Be open and honest, and things happen.

LISTEN FOR IT

I've learned to listen for passion in people. I can figure out what drives anyone. Passion is my drug of choice, but it doesn't have to be *my* passion. If I have a client who is beyond excited about something and has a great story behind it, I can get caught up in her passion and transfer it into my work. That kind of shared enthusiasm works extremely well in business.

Several years ago, my team got a call from a new client in New York. My people are terrific at new business calls like this, but this time my assistant put him on hold, buzzed me and said, "Look, I've got this guy on the line. There's something off. Can you jump on the call and take a listen?"

I love being on the front lines as much as I can, so without hesitating I picked up the phone and said, "Hey, how are you? This is Steve Sims. How can I help?"

The voice on the phone was one of the least enthusiastic I've ever heard. Which is weird in my line of business. People call us to help make their wildest dreams happen, so usually we get people who are pretty fired up about their requests.

However, this guy says, in monotone, "I need to get two tickets to the Playboy Mansion."

I said, "That's fine. We can make that happen for you. Let me get a pen so I can take some notes." I didn't need a pen, I needed to stall for a second, so I could think of a way to find this man's real reason for calling.

So I start chatting with him, "Have you been to the Playboy Mansion before?"

"No, no I haven't." And there's still no excitement in this young man's voice about going to The Capital of Hedonism. None at all.

"Do you get to Los Angeles much?" I asked, just chit-chatting.

"Yeah, sometimes."

"Where do you go? North? South? Just stay in the hub?"

"Well, I like Hollywood, but I usually go up to Santa Barbara," and I could sense the voice was picking up in tempo.

So, I said, "You like Santa Barbara?"

"Oh, yeah, I love Santa Barbara."

"Really? I've been there a couple times," I commented. "It was okay, I guess. What do you like so much about it?"

"Oh, well, the wine is incredible. . ." he said, and I could hear that he was smiling.

"Well, if you like wine, why aren't you heading up to Napa?" I asked.

That got him. "Oh, my God, I want to go to Napa so bad!" he said, almost like a little kid. And there it is. There's the excitement. There's the life on the line. Whew, I thought to myself, relieved. This, I can work with.

"Okay," I say, "we can send you to the Playboy Mansion, but first I really want to know why you haven't been to Napa?"

"Oh, I don't know! I always wanted to go to Napa." The guy was busting at the seams.

I thought to myself, I've *got* to get this guy to Napa. But I had to go through the original request protocol, so I went back to the Playboy project.

I ran through the planning for him. "We'll get you and a friend to the Playboy Mansion, you're at the Playboy Mansion for one night, let's look at your calendar."

He switched back to half-hearted right away.

When we were done scheduling, I said, "All right, back to Napa." And he perked up again.

It was like flicking a switch on and off. The second I mentioned Playboy, we were in the shits. Mention Napa, the guy was up on cloud nine. Then it hit me. The real him came out when he was talking about Santa Barbara and Napa and wine, but not about Playboy.

So, I asked, still chit-chatting, "What do you do for work?"

He said, "I'm a broker here in New York. I do this, I do that."

I said, "Got it. Now, I'm gonna go out on a limb here. And I mean no offense, and I have only acceptance, but, are girls not really your thing? And damn, mate, why the hell do you want to go to Playboy?"

He fell quiet for a moment and I thought he was going to hang up on me. I was challenging him to be authentic with me, and that's not an easy thing for people to do.

He said finally, "I get so much peer pressure. I have to do something that is pure 100 percent testosterone."

I understood. I was rolling now. He was being sincere, and so now I could sincerely help. "So the Playboy Mansion thing is not for you," I said. "You're doing it for everyone else in your office. Just to make them think you're straight. Is that it?"

"Yeah," he said softly.

"So you're gonna fly over to LA and spend about fifteen to twenty thousand dollars, just to hopefully placate a few assholes in your office?" I asked, incredulous.

"Apparently." He sounded defeated. I couldn't take it.

So, I said, "I've got an idea for you. We're going to send you to Napa. Because that's where your heart is. I've already got a few people going to the Playboy Mansion, so I'll get you a couple of ticket stubs. You'll fly back from

Napa with the ticket stubs, lay them on your desk, and no one's the wiser."

He was over the moon. We made that happen for him, and he became a client for many, many more years to come. Not because we sent him to Napa that one time, but because we listened to him and asked why. (Remember, ask why at least three times!)

That call was important training for me. I learned to listen for passion in others, and I learned to question them if their passion isn't showing. The more questions you ask, and if you're listening not just to the words but to the spark behind the answers, you'll be able to talk to people and find out what their passion is.

Sadly, we don't talk to ourselves enough to discover what our own passions are. We don't listen to ourselves, either. It took me a long time to have any idea where my passion was. Remember when I thought that working the door at clubs was going to get me a banking career? Oy.

QUESTION EVERYTHING

Do not believe what people tell you.

I'm not saying that they are liars, but most don't have the ability to communicate effectively. All of their best information is unsaid, somewhere between the lines.

It's like the guy I sent to Napa. You've got to be a bit of a psychologist. You've got to challenge them to give you the real answers.

I once called a tire company and said, "Hey, I want to order these tires for my bike." The guy said okay, and started putting in the request and processing the sale. There were no questions coming back at me. That's not Bluefishing. Bluefishing would have been if the guy at the tire place challenged my request. It would have gone something like this: "I've got those tires here, no problem, but real quick, can you tell me why you want them?" And I'd probably say, "Well, I heard they were the best. . . ." Then he'd say: "Well, where are you riding? What bike are the tires going on? How many miles do you do? Let me ask you a few more questions so that I can better understand what you're asking for, so maybe I can give you some other alternatives that are more targeted to your experience." That would have been a solid sale at any price, because I would have felt the tire salesman was invested and interested in me.

That's the person you want to become.

Little Bluefish who want to be Big Bluefish: the simple trick of the trade to stand out is to *question everything*. Start with yourself. Then move along to everything else you do, and those who are doing it, and those who are doing it for you.

QUESTIONING DOES NOT
EQUAL DOUBTING

So few people in this world will challenge or question a request. We live in an on-demand, service-driven world where whatever someone wants to buy, they usually can. You want plane tickets to Venice, you buy them. We're not used to the Bluefishing way of service, which is to challenge the request itself. A master Bluefisher would say back to you: You want to go away for the week? Okay, great! But why? Are you escaping from the kids so you can sleep and recharge? Are you looking to reconnect with your husband or wife? Do you want to learn a new skill somewhere? What has to happen to make this *the* week of all weeks?

The point is to drill quickly to the core. You want to question your way down to that single hot button, the thing that makes them tick. Then you connect on a level you've never connected before. Then you're in the most generous kind of service industry possible, because you're working on making something happen that is truly unique to them.

I'm not suggesting you become a Doubting Thomas prick when someone comes to you with a request. Questioning is not the same as doubting. I'm saying that you work on being the opposite, like you value their opinion more than anything else. When you do that, it makes you stand out like a lightbulb in the dark.

If you can challenge your communication with someone, you in essence challenge the relationship that you'll experience as well. If you can get into that person's head and get beyond the shield, beyond the business card, beyond the pomp and ceremony, beyond the ego, beyond the fear of embarrassment, then you can deliver for them like never before. There's a person that wakes up, lives and breathes, feeds, goes to the toilet, loves their kids, and this essence is what they want. Once you can see *that* person, once you've got them, they don't go anywhere else. It's not because they like your flashy website, it's not because of the overuse of punctuation, it's because you're communicating at a level they don't find anywhere else. Their passion is your language.

PASSION IS A LANGUAGE

Now, I know what my passion is. It's getting stuff done. It's my family, my motorcycles, my dogs, and it's drinking fine whiskey. But that doesn't mean I'm out of ideas when I get a client who wants to go to Napa and discover the best wines, which I personally don't drink. If it's real, even if it's not something I'm personally interested in, I can absolutely understand their passion.

And once I do, I can use their passion, and transfer it over to the people I'm dealing with to get them to open up other doors.

It's a communication knack that all Bluefishers have. You should look at passion as the best language or currency. If you want to be successful at anything, you need others to help you make things happen. Absolutely no one can do everything himself or herself. If you go in looking for how you can deal in passion, and how you can benefit the other person for a real win-win, you got it. That's negotiating with a great advantage.

In business, especially, it's important to identify your own passion right alongside someone else's. You can place these things in two columns, either on paper or in your head.

In one column there is your own passion. Understand what that is. Then, in the next column, write down the other person's passion. Understand how to connect with theirs. When you can get both working side by side, that tide floats all ships.

If there's no passion, there's no point. That will be the thing they write on my grave. If they don't, I will come back and engrave it myself.

SECRETS FROM
THE BLUEFISHING PLAYBOOK

★ Passion is something you have to discover. Relax. Try stuff. It takes time. But never stop looking.

★ If you knew that the Earth was going to collide with Mars tomorrow, what would you do right now? Maybe that's your passion.

★ Do not believe what people tell you. Most don't have the ability to communicate effectively. All of their best information is unsaid, somewhere between the lines. Drill down for it.

★ Actually give a damn. If *you* don't believe in it, *they* won't believe in it.

SIX

FAILURE IS JUST
MORE DISCOVERY

I'm a great believer that you should get out there and try things.

There are a lot of people who will overthink rather than overdo. Too many people out there think that to do something, they have to analyze the strategy, the costs, the projections. What they tend to do is build up an analytical report on 20,000 smart reasons why everything is going to fail, rather than one glistening reason why it's going to work.

Have you ever sat down on a Monday morning to plan your week? You get it all organized, day to day, hour to hour, and your to-do list is a work of art. After that, you're feeling so good about how on top of things you are that you head out for lunch, maybe you call a friend for a chat, then come back and pull up your list to start your day. That's when you glance at the clock and it's almost time to head out to get the kids or run to a meeting. You haven't gotten a single thing done. Where did your day go? You killed it by overplanning it and overthinking it.

Or take the usual story of a startup founder who needed to raise a round of financing. He researched one hundred investors in his area who might be interested in his space. Then he looked up all the other companies they had invested in. Then he gathered a list of those founders and their LinkedIn profiles and researched every last one of them. Then he created a pitch deck for each of those founders and went to lunch with many of them, thinking that if he could get them to introduce him onward, he would have a warmer intro to the investors he wanted to meet. He made a list of all the questions he thought each of his target investors would ask him and what their objections might be. You know what happened? By the time he had perfected his approach to investors, his company was nearly out of money, a competitor launched, and his employees, panicked, started to leave the company. He went out of business before he even pitched a single investor. He was so afraid of getting rejected by investors that he overanalyzed and overprepared. He did nothing, and that was his undoing.

IT'S NOT ABOUT YOUR IQ, IT'S ABOUT YOUR *I CAN*

What I do is look at something, take a small piece of what I'm looking at, and try it out to see if it works. If it fails, I just taught myself how not to do it. So I try it again, with a different approach. It fails, great, now I've learned *two* things about how not to do that project. That's what my kind of research looks like.

When I'm putting on a big event for a client, I don't need to know how to do the whole event. It's not important. The first thing I need to know is which things I can't do. The next thing is to find those people who can do what I can't. I just find the ones who are good enough at doing what I can't to make me look brilliant.

Kickstarter and Indiegogo and other crowdfunded sites are great platforms for testing whether there's a marketplace. Get a concept and put it out there. It is such a cheap, cheap way of researching whether anyone even wants what you make.

I love the way the Internet helps you see quickly whether an idea of yours has wings. You post something somewhere and someone writes, "I like that or I hate it." That's a crystal-clear, immediate gut reaction to the thing you'd proposed. The Internet has given us the ability to get an instant reaction, usually *before* we've sunk a ton of time and money into making the thing.

It doesn't matter if your first Kickstarter campaign crashes and burns. You can use that research to work out where you're going wrong. Do another campaign, put it up, wait a couple months, put another one up. Maybe change the font, change the colors, change the layout, change the description—and maybe it's still the same product.

Test marketing an idea is very valuable. It's not what you're thinking about it that matters. It's what a hundred or a thousand other people think. You may have a brilliant product, but you may be selling it to the wrong people. Or you may need to tweak your product to get it right for the right people. Maybe you weren't reaching the right clientele with the right tone of voice.

THE RESTAURATEUR
WHO CAN'T COOK

I knew a guy who wanted to open a restaurant. He wanted to do it "with everything in his heart." That's a winning ingredient, no doubt. But he had no money, he was fresh out of school, and guess what—he couldn't cook.

I asked him why the hell he thought he was going to open the best restaurant in the world. I wasn't trying to be a jerk. I genuinely wanted to know where his passion came from, and how he was going to put it to use. I challenge people so they can challenge themselves. I want them to answer the tough questions because if they can't come back with answers, it's not meant to be. I know a lot of Silicon Valley and Hollywood investors who do the same thing. The good ones, at least.

In this case, I told the guy to invite ten people over and cook for them. He needed to see if he could handle the rush. Then, at the end of the meal, he had to survey them. Whatever they said, he needed to hear. His friends might say his food is horrible, but that doesn't mean he has to give up his dream. He's just learning what he can't do.

Not every restaurant owner can cook. You may love the idea of opening up a restaurant. Maybe you're exceptional at orchestrating a team. In that case, you go find a phenomenal chef to do the cooking. Then you go and find a designer to design your restaurant. And waitstaff who know how to make customers feel taken care of. You don't have to be able to chop the potatoes yourself. You don't have to set the table. You just need to be able to magnificently orchestrate those who can.

I'm not saying that young guy with the restaurant dream will fail. No, and that's the whole point.

I want to find another word for *fail*. I don't believe that it means "not succeeding."

The Thai language has no direct translation of the English word *no*. The have a word for *yes* and for *try* but they don't have a common word for no. I think we should find an alternative word for the word *fail*. When you try and fail, the word should be *discover*.

When you're trying to create good food, but it doesn't taste good, you've just discovered you need to add more salt. If you try to set the table and everyone complains, "We're jam-packed in here, no one can put their arms out," you just discovered how to set the table properly.

If you want to open a restaurant, and you're that kid with no money, and no ability to cook, I want to know why we should back you, why should we believe in you? Why you? I want you to be able to challenge yourself to be able to come back with a good answer. If you can, the rest of it is systematically easy.

So, go discover some stuff about what you want to do. If you want to get sand in your toes, you hang out at a beach. If you want to open a restaurant, get your ass in a restaurant. Eat in good restaurants and discover what you like about each one. Talk to everyone who works there and listen to what they say about it. Go work in a restaurant yourself and learn from the inside out what makes one restaurant better than the next. Discover what you don't know and learn to do it. There's no failure in this at all.

FAILURE IS PAYING FOR AN EDUCATION

Let's say you start your first business. You make a really great product, but no customers turn up and you run out of cash. Hey, you just discovered accounting and marketing. You didn't fail. You learned what to do on your next attempt. And you know what? You just paid for an education.

You pay for college to learn how to do things. Right? You pay for classes so you can learn something. Going into business is the exact same as paying for courses in college. If your business doesn't work out, you just paid for those classes on how to do better design, better marketing, better lead generation, better engineering, better project management, better personal hiring. You are constantly being educated.

I want to delete the words *fail* and *failure* from your language.

If I said to you, "I discovered how not to build that motorcycle," I'm operating from a position of learning and improving. But if I told you, "I failed at building that motorcycle," well, that's finite. That's the end. My end result was that I failed. It's over.

If you try to open a shop and it doesn't work, it's a bust, no one turns up, and to say that it failed is the end of that dream. But to say that you discovered so many things you couldn't do, that's an education on the next step.

Changing your perspective from failing to discovering is what allows you to continue to the next leg of your journey. It gives you both the courage and the curiosity to keep going.

There's no end of the road until you're six feet under.

THERE ARE NO OBSTACLES, NONE AT ALL

When you're an entrepreneur, you need to be able to weather the rejection, disdain, and every *no* placed in front of you. You've got to be inoculated against any form of reality imposed by anyone else. Remember, no passion, no point. Many things can be enhanced, rented, and outsourced, but that passion cannot.

When you're having a bad day, or things aren't quite going right, you'll notice that other things come along that derail your focus. That's when you employ one of the most self-defeating observations on the planet, "I'm having one of those days!"

It is absolutely critical, when you feel like that, that you learn how to break away from that negative place and go do something you're passionate about. Even just for twenty minutes. Do the opposite of the negative. Do something pure fun. Do that, then come back to the work at hand. Those same obstacles you thought were guillotines just an hour ago, guess what? You can't even recognize them anymore. They're no longer hurdles for you; they're not even speed bumps. You go straight through them because passion gives you a turbocharge to get through those obstacles. You don't perceive obstacles when you're in this zone.

How much you believe in your own project is critical to whether it will be successful or not. Authenticity and passion are parallel. They go hand in hand. You can't have one without the other. You absolutely cannot. But when you have them both, that's a double whammy.

Now, pair those with your new discovery mindset. You don't fear failure, because there is no failure, just the chance to discover more about how to do something. Authenticity, passion, and a commitment to do and discover. That's a phenomenal tank to roll into any battle with.

In this mindset there are no obstacles. There are zero obstacles at all. Obstacles are self-invented. .

I'm serious. This isn't just cheerleading talk. This is Bluefishing.

Obstacles are only in your mind. They are like a prophecy that you fulfill just to make your failure feel better. And I purposely use the word *failure* now, because if you build up those obstacles in your head, you're looking for a reason to end it. That's where that failure comes in.

You're not a loser or a failure if you get knocked down. We all get knocked down. As they say, the fight's not over when you go down. The fight's over when you stop getting up.

SECRETS FROM
THE BLUEFISHING PLAYBOOK

★ Failure is just an education in what not to do. For every failure, you're learning. Take pride in your scars.

SEVENTH-INNING STRETCH

RELAX, YOU'RE IN GOOD COMPANY

You've probably heard that Walt Disney got turned down over 300 times when he was seeking financing for Disneyland. Or that Colonel Sanders got turned down over 1000 times for his now world-famous chicken recipe.

Now, I am positive that, after one thousand rejections, Mrs. Sanders was saying, "You've got to get another job, fellow, because this ain't selling."

And yet the Colonel carried on.

Stupere is a Latin word meaning stunned. That's where the word *stupid* comes from. It really means "stunned, dazed, amazed."

This is a key secret to how Bluefishers make things happen. We are stupified by our own powerful possibilities. An ignorance of failure drives us. It is inconceivable that what we want is not going to happen. Inconceivable.

I'm not saying to be delusional and unintelligent. I'm saying that when you fixate on a goal and know passionately that you can reach it, then spending a single second thinking that it won't work is just a massive waste of time.

I can't begin to tell you how much I love this idea. I want you to get stupid. Get stunned. And forget that failure is even possible.

I'm going to give you a list of people who learned to cut the word *failure* from their vocabularies. This doesn't mean they didn't get rejected, laughed at, judged or humiliated. They did. Thousands of times. Everyone has felt that way, I promise you. These people just didn't let that stop them.

The truth is rarely what we think it is. Failure is not failure; it's discovery. What people think about you is their perception, it's not a fact about you. Walls can be knocked down. (And maybe they only existed in your head to begin with).

The Bluefishers who realize all this—realize that so much more is possible than their current circumstances—they are the ones who really take it to the next level.

Dog-ear this page and come back to it when you feel

that your dream is impossible. You are not alone. You're in great company.

Don't quit.

A SHORT LIST OF PEOPLE
WHO DIDN'T GIVE UP

* Stephen King threw away his first novel, *Carrie*, after it was rejected thirty times. His wife fished it out of the trash.

* Henry Ford went broke five times and was advised to stay out of the auto industry because he didn't have the money or the know-how.

* Albert Einstein didn't speak until he was four, or read until he was seven. Teachers said he wouldn't amount to much.

* Annapolis rejected Dwight Eisenhower.

* James Dyson had 5,126 nonworking bagless vacuum prototypes and no more savings. He's worth $4.5 billion now.

* USC rejected Steven Spielberg three times.

* Van Gogh sold hardly any paintings in his lifetime.

* Walt Disney got turned down over 300 times for financing Walt Disney World. He was also fired

from a newspaper for having no original ideas. Or imagination.

* Steve Jobs was removed from the company he started.

* Michael Jordan was cut from his high school basketball team.

* After his role in *American Graffiti,* Harrison Ford had to go back to carpentry. Then, *Star Wars* happened.

* Five record companies passed on The Beatles.

* Bill Gates is a college dropout.

* Mark Twain went bankrupt.

* Twenty-seven publishers rejected Dr. Seuss's first book.

* "Unfit for television," Oprah was fired from a reporting job because she was too emotionally invested in her stories. She eventually became the host of *The Oprah Winfrey Show,* which aired for twenty-five seasons.

* Pete Athans learned how not to climb Everest his first four times, and went on to do it seven.

* Meryl Streep almost quit after a director said she was too ugly.

* Elvis was told he should go back to truck driving.

* J. K. Rowling was a single mother on welfare. And the first billionaire author.
* Winston Churchill wasn't a good student, he stuttered, and his parents ignored him.
* Abraham Lincoln lost eight elections.
* Beethoven's teacher said he was a hopeless composer.

EIGHT

BE AFRAID OF STANDING STILL

We are all born unique, then spend the next forty years diluting ourselves to become just like everyone else. Think about it. If you're using 80 percent of your energy or effort to be someone you're not, then you can only ever give 20 percent of *you*. But if you're just you, there is zero effort involved in that. When you turn up as 'you,' whomever 'you' are, people just seem to like you better. Because you're not a fake. People can see right through that.

Let's say, for example, that you're in a middle-management job at an insurance firm. You show up for work on your first day, and you see four hundred desks in this giant office, but only a few corner offices to get promoted to. What do you do? Well, of course you have to do the best work you can, but that's not enough. You also have to stand out, and the easiest way to stand out is by being yourself.

The problem is that standing out is scary. Sticking your neck out there for other people to judge you is frightening. Here's the thing you have to understand. The worst thing in the world is not that you'll try something and get knocked down or laughed at. The worst thing that could possibly happen is to be *exactly in the same spot* a year from now, just one person among four hundred, doing the same thing this year and next year and the year after that, standing still.

ALTER THE POINT OF FEAR

So many so-called leaders and gurus say that we should be fearless. That's just not possible. If you're human, you've been afraid. Maybe you're afraid of something right now. That's normal. It's part of how we're all made.

It's a great thing to be scared. In a moment of fear, all of your senses are heightened and you work at 200 percent. The adrenaline kicks in and you are *in*. In that moment, you are hyper-focused, and no one can get in your way.

The problem is that people often use fear as their excuse for not going forward. Instead of letting fear stop you, what if you could learn to alter the point of the fear itself? Be fearful that in a month's time, you will be in exactly the same place that you are right now.

I believe that a lot of people stay in ruts because they're

comfortable. They know what the rut looks like. They know that, on Friday, they get one-thousand dollars, and they know that on Monday, eight hundred of it is gone to pay off bills. So, on Tuesday, they have two-hundred dollars left. They've got this rut, they've got this formula, they're in this system. It's survival, but that's it. To me, that is the scariest thing possible, because you're not growing. You're standing still.

When you're the guy whose house just burned down, when you fall off motorcycles, go bust, lose money or get screwed over, you really only have two choices. Those experiences can define you, or they can grow you. There are a lot of people (like in my dad's saying that you don't drown from jumping in water, you only drown if you stay in it too long), who dwell on the experience for too long, and use it as their excuse to stop.

THE THINGS THAT HAPPEN TO YOU ARE NOT YOUR OBITUARY

I live in California where there are the best motorcycle roads in the world, bar none. There's a place, Angel's Crest, in Glendale. It goes all the way up into the mountains and it goes so high, there's snow at the peak. It's a beautiful ride.

The downside is that during summer there are massive brush fires and the roads are closed for a few months. But the funny thing is, every September, when you go back through Angel's Crest, after the grisliest fires have destroyed hundreds of acres in June and July, there are these buds blooming and beautiful greenery everywhere you look. That ash created fertilizer for new growth. I see these amazing fires, and then growth that comes out of it, and it's my favorite ride on Earth. It always reminds me that things that happen to you are not your obituary.

It's the fear of standing still that drives me. I look at things and think, "I want to try that." Then I ask myself, "Well, what's the outcome?" The outcome is if I try and succeed, I succeed. Great. If I try and fail, I'll grow. Also great. If I don't try at all, I'll have allowed something to get in my way, or I'll have missed tasting something that I could have grown from. I will be standing still.

Everything stagnant rots. If you're not growing, you're dying.

GET COMFORTABLE BEING UNCOMFORTABLE

Back when I was just getting started and was stranded in Hong Kong, I had no money, no future, no ideas, not a clue. Honestly, I wasn't too bothered by it. I just thought,

"Well, I've had no money. I've had no job. I've had no plans. So, there you go. I'm used to this."

That's how I realized I was already comfortable with being uncomfortable. It's much more natural for me to be uncomfortable, because it means I'm trying something new. It gets the wheels turning. It gives me an occasion to rise to. Maybe it applies to the thrill seeker in me. The competitor. The guy who likes to go out and discover new lands.

I live in the hills of Hollywood. I'm in a spot where no one can see me, no one can find me, and a lot of people don't even know that there is a house up here. One of the things that I fell in love with when I came up to this house was a palm tree. It's so freaking tall and when it gets windy up here in the hills, it just sways back and forth, sometimes softly, sometimes violently. The tree was made that way, it was made to take the beating and endure the changing winds. As long as it doesn't try to resist, it overcomes. A rigid, stiff tree would break in those winds, but not my tree.

It was an especially windy day the first time I visited this house with the tall swaying palm tree. I instantly thought, "I'm that tree. I'm comfortable with being uncomfortable. I don't mind getting a couple smacks in the head. I know I'm gonna get back up again." This tree is one of the reasons I bought the house.

For me, the real thing I'm terrified of is monotony. I'm the guy who jumps into the water, then wonders if it's cold. I fuck up, I overextend, I overreach constantly, and it goes wrong so many times. However, when it goes wrong, I always know that I can wake up the following day and I can make it right, because it's happened before.

After jumping into so many pools of water, some cold, some hot, some scalding, some with no water in them at all, I've become confident in my resilience to be able to overcome my own errors.

SECRETS FROM
THE BLUEFISHING PLAYBOOK

★ It's not about your IQ. It's about your I Can.

★ Everything stagnant rots. If you're not growing, you're dying.

★ What happens to you is not your obituary. Get back up again, Bluefisher.

★ Don't be afraid of change. Be afraid of standing still.

NINE

UGLY WORKS

There's a word that I'm actually starting to dislike: *Authentic*. It's overused. Actually being authentic is great, but the minute authentic becomes a marketing adjective, it's no longer real. So I describe what I do in a different way now. My whole focus is that I try not to do things that are too polished. I'm a great believer that the more unpolished something is, the more natural it is. People are getting to the point at which they distrust what they see, because people and companies on the Internet are getting better and better at manufacturing a relationship with you, or pretending to understand your interests. People just want something *real*. We need something to believe in.

Think about it. Everything that we see is CGI or made up or touched up or filtered, and it doesn't really look like that. We're constantly bombarded with photos of pretty people and pretty things that we know are not real. There will be a picture of a huge, tempting dessert on a menu, and when we order it, it's nothing like what was on the menu and it's about the size of a bottle cap. Every phone camera now has an enhance button or a so-called beauty mode for selfies. Everyone is messed with for marketing's sake.

The simple fact, however, is that we yearn for something that's not perfect. Cindy Crawford was one of the greatest supermodels, and she hit the stratosphere of success because she had a clear flaw. She had the mole. She could have had it removed, and I read somewhere that she was told to do so, but she smartly refused. I believe it was that mole, that slight technical imperfection that gave her that special, uniquely gorgeous, look.

Have you ever seen Picasso's early works? The early, early, early stuff? He was pretty much imitating everybody else. His stuff was very Renaissance. The women looked like women, and the boys looked like boys. He did proper paintings. He never got anywhere until he started sticking two eyeballs on one side and two ears on the other side. That's when Picasso became Picasso, because he created imperfections. That's what makes people look twice. That's what makes them talk about it.

Then you've got Jackson Pollock who just threw his paint on the canvas. When most people see a Pollock, they think, "There's energy, there's life!" We all like to see things that are raw.

This is why a cornerstone of my personal brand and ethos, and a rule of Bluefishing too, is that, "Ugly works."

My definition of *ugly* is this: Unpolished. Raw. Not overproduced. Real. And I don't like it when people over-use this word: *Authentic*.

Let me show you what I mean.

PERFECTLY IMPERFECT

With the huge amount of email we get now, there is less actual paper mail cluttering our mailboxes at home. Even five years ago, when I'd check my mail, I'd have twenty envelopes in there every day. Now, there are maybe two or three. This is why I love to send a letter, handwritten, with a stamp. You can't type, it because then it could have been automated. You can't create a perfect crease in the fold of the letter, because then it could have come from a fulfillment center. You just fold it over once, give it a quick squeeze, and shove it in an envelope. There. Now a human being has obviously sent it.

This is how I get people to know that it's really me

sending them something. It's messy on purpose. Under-produced. *Ugly*. It goes against the grain, so it's perfectly imperfect. This isn't just zigging when others zag in order to stand out. This is standing out by being real.

A piece of mail is a very small thing. That's the whole point. Small, creative, ugly (not polished) methods work to get someone's attention.

There was a guy I needed to meet on behalf of a client. I started the same way anyone would; I spent some time Googling and reading about him. I found out that he was really into vintage Porsches. A day later, when I was at a gas station, I popped into the mini-mart and noticed a magazine called *The Best Old Cars* or something like that. In it, there was an article about a vintage Porsche. I could send the magazine to this guy with a line like, "Hey, hope you like the magazine. I know you love Porsches. When can we have a chat?" But then I thought, let's get a little more creative. How can this add mystery, intrigue, interest? So I ripped out the page and ripped it in half, showing only half the Porsche. Half a page. I folded that up in the envelope. I wrote on the page, "You get the rest when we get the chance to meet."

I got the meeting and took the magazine along with me. Now, I'm sure he didn't care about it at all. It's not like he was desperate to get a free magazine out of me. But the way I approached him worked and caught his attention.

SKYMALL, SELFIES, AND BAR TABS

Here are a few more examples of small, creative, ugly stuff that I like to do to make a connection with another person.

I love SkyMall catalogues. You know, the ones with Tyrannosaurus Rex mailboxes and skeleton-hand back scratchers. Fun, stupid, ugly stuff. Whenever I fly, I try to grab as many of those magazines as I can. They have so many pages that I can rip out. (*Rip* is a key word. Don't slice it with a razor blade; rip it out and get a big fat Sharpie.) Then, I take one of those pages and do something like write to a client, "I hear you're moving to your new house. I think a T-Rex mailbox is exactly what you need for your new place." Fold it up, put it in there, write on the envelope, mail it.

It conveys a sense of humor and an attention to detail. While he may not want a Tyrannosaurus Rex mailbox out front, he is aware that you were thinking about him and that you remembered that he's in a new home. It makes him smile because nobody else is doing this.

Here's another idea. Make a selfie video with your

phone and email it over to someone you need to talk to. "Hey, Peter, I know you're busy, but I wanted to chat with you, so I shot this twenty-three second video to speak to you about so-and-so. Can we continue the conversation?"

Or, how about this one? When I'm staying at a hotel, I always ask for a bunch of stationery and envelopes, and I write a few letters. A few days later, a client gets an envelope in the mail with a hotel logo on it and goes, "Who the hell do I know that just stayed at the Standard in Miami?" She opens it up, and there's a personal note from me on the hotel stationery, saying "Hey, Allison, I was just catching up on some work from my hotel in Miami, and I wanted to send you a note because I've been meaning to reach out to you. Can I call you next Tuesday?" Just something like that. It's so simple.

A HANDWRITTEN LETTER BEATS AN EMAIL EVERY TIME

The other beautiful thing about writing letters is that you're not looking at a screen. When you're looking at a screen, reading an email, what's happening on the rest of the screen? Other emails are coming in, other messages are pinging up in the corner, and you're distracted. However, with my ugly method, when you're opening an envelope, you're more engaged because your body is moving, your hands are ripping something up, you're looking at it, you bring it out, you unfold it. There's a lot of physical and mental engagement in opening up a letter, as opposed to reading an email, which is one click away from getting deleted.

Whenever I mail something to someone, like a book or a magazine, I always do it in some kind of different wrapping paper. My favorite is the old brown butcher's paper. If you want to get creative, tie a piece of string around it. People don't get stuff that looks like that.

Here's another thing I like to do. When I go to a bar and have a drink, I always ask for a copy of the receipt. I write on the back of it something like, "Hank, I'm here drinking whiskey and thinking about the project we are working on. Just wanted to let you know I was thinking of you. All the best, Steve." Then I mail Hank the receipt. This one always get a chuckle, and most clients ask when they're going to get my next bar tab in the mail.

I'm part of a travel agency group, and they create a big book at the end of every year, called *Best of the Best.* It's a really nicely thick, card-covered book with incredible photos of different hotels throughout the world. It's nothing more than a big, glitzy magazine, but it's about

350 pages and it feels special. We used to send them out directly from the fulfillment center, wrapped in a plastic sleeve with the customer's name and address on it, already printed and costing us no postage. It went out every year and we'd send an email following up, "Hey, client, did you get the book?" "Yeah, I did, thanks a lot."

So, we tried an experiment. We got fifty of these books, and I recruited my daughter and told her friends' parents: "Come on over, I'll pay your kids five dollars to wrap these books. It's good for them." We didn't want things to be perfect. We wrapped the books in any kind of wrapping paper the kids like. We handwrote the envelopes. Then we sent them out. So, it was now costing us time, yeah, and it was costing us extra postage, which we didn't have to worry about prior to that.

But we got so much business out of that. Clients were contacting us first, instead of us contacting them, just to say things like: "Great book! My wife loves this!" Seven days after fifty books were mailed out, we had booked sixty hotel rooms for different clients.

Of course, none of this works if you overuse it. You're not going to write a letter for every business communication, otherwise you'd get no business done. You're not going to send a package to every client, to every person you wish you could meet. But when you pick the right time to do it, it is a way of getting through the snowstorm of technology messaging.

I've never understood why we're not all that ugly.

BLUEFISHERS KNOW HOW TO ADAPT QUICKLY

When Napoleon wanted to honor a special dinner guest, do you know what the cutlery was made of? Not silver. Not gold. Aluminum.

Going further back in time, when Emperor Tiberius, one of Rome's greatest generals, was presented with an aluminum plate by a goldsmith who claimed it was rarer than gold, instead of saying thanks, do you know what the emperor did? He had the man's head cut off. Tiberius knew that if a shiny new metal got onto the market, his stockpile of silver and gold would be totally devalued.

All this over a metal we now use for rain gutters.

Why did aluminum used to be so valuable? Because it was the rarest material at the time. It was so rare because there was no way of being able to excavate it and melt it down. Because of how hard it was to make pliable, that effort and rarity made it worth something. As soon as we found a way to excavate aluminum, melt it down, and use it in just anything, its rarity was lost.

This is a story to illustrate not just that being your unique, hard-to-clone self is incredibly valuable, but also that what things are important today will not necessarily be important next week. What tools or tricks we used to great benefit last week might just be noise and fluff next week. I'm perfectly aware that all the funny ways I have described for being ugly and raw and real might fall flat in a year. My thoughts on social media and Likes and CGI might get outdated real quick. That's okay. Those are all just tactics. But the *idea*, this mindset of being unpolished and personal and real and true, that won't ever change. Not for a skilled Bluefisher.

Bluefishing is about being able to adapt your techniques. First, you have to be able to question what is in front of you, listen in between the lines, and keep trying unique, standout ways to make a genuine connection with someone. Then you can and should evolve the tools and tricks you use.

SECRETS FROM
THE BLUEFISHING PLAYBOOK

★ A handwritten note beats an email every single time: It takes less than a second to delete an email, but a minimum of three minutes (and a lot more emotion) to discard something real.

★ Let people know you're thinking about them. It goes far.

★ "Ugly" works. For Bluefishers, ugly means raw, unpolished, quick, and real. It's the opposite of overpolished, CGI, and corporate.

TEN

PERSONAL BRANDING IS PERSONAL (IMAGINE THAT)

Everyone you see is hard at work on their own personal branding. The boy at school who wants to be the cool kid is doing it. The sixteen-year-old who makes herself up so guys will think she's older, she's doing personal branding. So is the software engineer wearing sneakers, a hoodie, and a pair of jeans. So is the rock star in a leather jacket, long hair, and tattoos on her arms.

It's an irony I don't understand. Every person and brand wants to be special, to carve out their own niche, and to be identified as a standalone personal product. How do they do it? Well, the first thing they do is dress the part. They try to fit into the profile of what they think they should be, what everyone else does. While being unique is exactly what they were before they started. You're born unique.

I want those people to realize that personal branding isn't about what you wear or who you hang out with. It's not about trying on different layers and different personas to conform with what you think other people expect. It's about taking an honest, Bluefish-style look at yourself to figure out what your core persona is.

I LEARNED HOW TO BE ME
THE HARD WAY

These days, I am completely comfortable just being Steve Sims. When you interact with me, whether it's for business or bringing me waffles at the diner, I'm just a big British guy and you're just chatting with me. That's the only way I can get stuff done the way I do, because I don't have to waste a second of energy being anyone other than myself.

But I learned this the hard way. I spent a lot of time trying to hide the fact that I was a bricklayer's son from East End in London, that I grew up poor, and didn't have what a lot of the rich people around me had. As soon as I started making money, real money for the first time in my life, I quickly let money be my voice. I fell into the "what I'm supposed to look like" trap. So much peer pressure told me that I couldn't be taken seriously just as

I was, just as Steve Sims, and I felt as though it was time to grow up. The way I went about it was to dress myself in layer after layer of shields. I wore the suit, the expensive loafers, the designer belt; not for my benefit, but for yours.

Here's what happened. I created my own disconnect. When I got near you, all dressed up like that, you got confused. Because once you started talking with me, you realized that my talk didn't match my walk. There was someone in front of you who wasn't one-hundred percent authentic, and something made you think, uneasily, "Something's not right about this guy." No one does business with people when that tiny alarm bell is saying something is not right.

For example, you call for a plumber to clear out your drains. Your doorbell rings, and the guy at the door has an expensive three-piece suit on, saying he's your plumber. Something inside you goes, "Eh, something's a bit funny here." You probably won't let him in the house.

When I started listening to peer pressure and became someone I wasn't, everything went wrong. Things started to spiral out of control. The financials started to slip but, prior to that, my relationships started to slip. That was the barometer that I quickly focused on. "Why am I not getting the phone calls back from people I used to hang out with? Why am I not communicating well? Why am I not connecting? Why am I not engaging with my friends anymore?"

That was when I went back to basics. I took off the suits and the fancy stuff. I went back to my black t-shirt and jeans. I went to meetings and parties like that, not there to impress anyone, just there to be me. All of a sudden people started gravitating back to me. "You know, there's a guy. He doesn't look like he's trying too hard, he's comfortable in his own skin." Confident people want to hang around confident people.

I didn't have to put in any effort to be someone else anymore, so I could put all that work into just being me. It was raw and unpolished and real. It was *ugly*. I like being Ugly Sims.

THE WORST PICTURE OF ME EVER TAKEN

Here's a little story to illustrate the depth of how wrong I got it for a while. I have a photograph of me from 1997. I'll be honest with you; it's a painful picture. I was in Monaco for Ferrari's fiftieth anniversary, doing a big deal event at the Monaco Grand Prix to celebrate. I had a little 1972 Ferrari Dino at the time. Beautiful car. I had also rented a yacht for the event, because it was easier to be closer to the action.

Naturally, I wanted to get a picture of me living it up in Monaco. So I put on my best suit, pulled up in my Ferrari, in front of my rented yacht, and my guy started snapping. We quickly realized, though, that the yacht next to us was two meters longer than the yacht I had rented, so we moved the car over and took the picture of me in front of the bigger yacht. (This was insane; I had rented a very big fucking yacht).

So that's the picture: Me in my suit looking very *Miami Vice*, leaning up against my Ferrari, posing like an asshole in front of some other person's yacht. I still have that photograph. I look at it and think, "Even with a yacht, a killer car, having been *personally invited* by Ferrari to the event in Monaco, you were still intimidated by what the next guy had."

It's a very painful reminder that I often look at to tell me: Sims, buddy, be happy with you and don't ever try, ever again, to gain credibility or love or lust or likes from anybody else. That approval isn't going to pay your mortgage, raise your kids, keep your marriage together or bring you any real joy.

We might not all have an actual photograph to hold and look at, but I'm pretty sure every one of us has a painful memory of trying to be someone they weren't, working hard for the validation of so many people who didn't matter.

REDEFINING WEALTH

About ten years ago, I was working in Palm Beach. That place was absolutely dripping in money. Everyone I was dealing with had $10-million houses and then some. If you had a $5-million-dollar house, you were second-rate. All these people bought their houses right on the main drag, not because it was the best street for them and their families, but because it was the place to be seen. They wanted everyone else to know that they could afford a $10-million house.

There was a lot of that kind of thing going on in Palm Beach. These people had the watches, the cars, the girl-friends, the yachts, and the country-club memberships, but before I could articulate it, I knew there was some-thing missing. These people were the searchers. They were not happy. They were not comfortable.

Then there was the guy who lived down the road. He had been married to his best friend for ten years, drove a car that he didn't owe any money on, his kids went to a good school, and came home safely every night. They were all fed and warm and together.

To me, *that* guy is wealthy.

I remember it being a massive breakthrough for me when I realized that many of the people I was dealing with back then had a lot of dollars, but no wealth.

For years I had tried to hide my own low-class neighborhood upbringing, thinking like so many other entrepreneurs coming from nothing that I needed to talk the Rolex talk to be accepted in business. Then, thanks to Palm Beach, I realized the difference between dollars and wealth.

My wealth wasn't based on how many high-end watches I could buy. It was based on knowing that whatever I was enduring and experiencing during the day, I could have total peace of mind going to sleep at night knowing that my children had been fed, my wife was safe and loved and that there was a roof over our heads.

These days I have a lot of toys, sure, but none of those things have anything to do with my wealth. My wealth is simply that I am me. I look after those around me, and I have love and support and faith with those people.

HOW DO YOU PERSONALLY BRAND?

It's time to do a self-audit. You may well be an asshole. You may be a real cretin. But if you're reading this book, you obviously want something better for yourself, so give yourself a break, okay? You've already taken the first step.

Now, in the audit, ask yourself, "What do I like? What don't I like? What kind of people do I like? What people don't I like?" Make two columns: Like and Don't Like. There's no use just making a list of "I like, I like, I like." For this to work, you have to be crystal clear about you. You have to see the bad stuff. This is your own sandbox that you can kick around in to figure yourself out. Be simplistic and blunt with yourself. And write it down. You've got to see the truth, right in front of your eyes.

Next, I want you to make another list. What are your principles? What are you good at, what are you bad at? It's those principles that develop a personal brand. Do I let people down? Do I get shit done? Do I know how to do great copy? Do I know how to write a good book? Am I lousy at returning emails? Do I like to travel? Do I lie to people to sound more interesting? Do I like curry? Just go on like this for a while. Be brutally honest with yourself. Don't worry: No one but you will ever see this list.

Now, take a look at your lists. You'll find plenty of things in there that you don't like about yourself, but you do them anyway, glaringly so. You'll easily see the things you need to start removing from your life. Because things don't magically get better.

In motorcycle mechanics, we always focus on the weakest link. How are your brake pads? Do you have air pressure? Is your chain tight? The simple stuff. We don't care if the camshafts are balanced, we don't care if the valve adjustment is correct. None of that stuff is going to stop us or kill us. If you go around a corner and the brakes don't work, that's going to kill you. Focus on the smallest element that can bring you down. Focus on your own weakest links, the things that foul up your life or your work again and again and again. This is the first step in strengthening your personal brand.

You want to look at yourself as your own brand, your own company. Why would I buy from this company? Why would I trust this brand? Why would I want to be a part of it? Imagine that you're looking for a new girlfriend or boyfriend. Why would anyone want to spend any time with you? They may be attracted to you at first but, after a few dates they're very quickly going to ask themselves, "Well, why do I want to go out again? Why should I give a bunch of my time to this person?"

Look at yourself and learn. "Okay. This is what I stand for. This is what I don't settle for. This is how I want people to feel when they're around me. This is how I feel I should be treated." When you identify that for yourself, you're building up your own persona, your own set of ideals, ideology, and personal branding.

You're already that person. You're already unique. You're you. This process will just help you develop your core persona, your personal brand. Once you can find that person and build him or her back up, you can explode with authenticity from there.

THE CHUG TEST

This is the simplest way in the world to figure out if someone is a good match for you as a business partner, client, friend, tutor, trainer, whatever.

I call it the Chug Test. If I'm walking down the sidewalk, and I see someone I know walking on the other side of the street, what do I do? This could be anyone in my life, a school friend, a client, an investor, my mailman, my dentist, absolutely anyone I know. Do I see them and run across the street, jump in front of them and go, "Bernard! How you doing? Let's go chug a beer!" Or do I look the other way, pretending I haven't noticed them, and pick up my pace to make a clean getaway? Simply, do I want to go and have a drink with that person or not? That's the Chug Test.

The Chug Test is what I used to make up my mind about the salesperson I had to fire. I said to Clare, my wife, who works with me, "I'm gonna keep it simple. I tell people about this Chug Test concept, but I'm not living by it if I keep her around in the company." Regardless of how much money she made for me and the company, regardless of whether the clients liked her, I honestly didn't. So I fired her. I literally fired one of my top performers because she didn't pass the Chug Test. You could look at it and think, "Oh, my God, Sims, you're an idiot, you just got rid of a big asset, why couldn't you just suck it up and ignore her and let her do her thing?" Or you could look at it and realize, "You got rid of something that was toxic to you, and anything toxic to you is toxic to the company."

The strange thing that happened was that the rest of my team was really respectful of the decision. I heard them saying things like, "I wasn't sure if Sims was ever going to do that." Behind the scenes they had been thinking to themselves, "Does he actually do what he says he does?" I was a bit stunned myself when I let her go, but my circle became better, my work relationships got stronger, and my reputation became more authentic: "Oh, Sims, he's not just talk. He walks the walk. He lives it."

This is so simple, it's almost silly. It has been my guide in life for so long. I'll interview clients for membership in Bluefish, and I'll use the Chug Test in my head to determine whether I want to take them on. I don't welcome a bad match even if it will make me rich. We were recently trying out a new accountant, and I asked my wife, who worked with him, "Would you chug a beer with him?" She quickly answered "No." So, I said, "There's billions of people on the planet, plenty of accountants to hire, go and find one you *would* have a beer with." My accountant I have now, I'd chug a beer with him.

DON'T WASTE YOUR TIME COUNTING LIKES

So many people are getting personal branding all wrong. They're putting unbelievable amounts of time and energy into their social media status, which is often bogus. I know it's bullshit. You know it's bullshit. The whole freaking planet knows it's bullshit, yet we still do it. We post something to Facebook or Instagram or Twitter, and then proceed to have a confidence meltdown when not enough people have liked it. It's exhausting.

I met a college kid who paid one company, so that

every time he posted to Facebook, he'd get five hundred people to like him because, he said, "It makes me look good." I said back to him, "How in the hell can five hundred people from the Philippines, whom you don't know and who don't know your friends, make you look like anything more than the dick you are who obviously bought five hundred likes?" He couldn't see the meaninglessness in it.

Don't get me wrong. I'm not by any means saying that social media is bad. There are amazing uses for it that bring people together in a real, actual way. Just don't waste your time looking at the Likes and followers since they all can be manipulated. I'd much rather have a Facebook post where I get ten people to respond with a real comment, than have three thousand people pushing Like, Like, Like. You see this a lot. You see a picture with a thousand Likes, but not one comment, not one single actual person has said, "That's cool" or "I like that color" or "Rock on!" Nothing like that, not one comment.

I believe you can have one million followers, but you only need ten to be super rich. This is going to sound harsh, and it might upset a lot of people I know, but the simple fact is that in my life, outside of my wife, I think I've got three friends. I honestly think I've got three people. Three people whose doors I could knock on, at one o'clock in the morning and go, "I'm fucked," and they would go, "Get a seat. Let's chat." Three people that I can phone and say, "I'm on the other side of the planet, but I just lost my wallet. I need to borrow your credit card. What are the numbers?" Three people that you never have to give excuses to. You don't have to be anyone else for them. Just you.

I predict we're going to experience a total reset of the social media schematic, as we did with the housing market. We're going to have a reset when the bubble is going to burst and you're going to see who will actually miss you if you're gone. You may think you have all these people, these thousands of followers, these online friends, but how many of them are actually part of your life?

This is different from business. We'll get to that. In business, there is a way to create a certain perception of your brand. In business, it's a powerful strategic position to be seen as the market leader, the most inspirational, the most direct, the person everyone reads and actually follows and quotes. What I'm talking about right now is personal branding (and once you learn this, you can do a much better job leading your business, too). You have to realize you cannot pay your bar tab with the number of likes you have on Facebook.

SECRETS FROM
THE BLUEFISHING PLAYBOOK

* Do a self-audit, because things don't magically get better. Take an honest look at your strengths and weaknesses. Invest in the strengths and see what weaknesses you need to remove.

* How do you walk into a room? Personal branding is not marketing and Twitter followers. It's figuring out your core persona. Who you are, not who they want you to be.

* Don't waste your time counting likes: You'll never be able to pay your bar tab with Facebook likes.

* Try the Chug Test. If you want to know if someone is a good match for you (as a client, customer, vendor, boss, employee, friend), ask yourself: Would I chug a beer with that person?

ELEVEN

THE POWER TO SAY NO

As we begin to come alive by Bluefishing, finding that new place of self-confidence, we often make the mistake of accepting *everything* and not filtering anything out. Many of us are so good at accepting challenges. As entrepreneurs, we're always saying "Sure! Gimme, gimme, gimme. I'll take it on. Yes I can do that." We've gotten good at something and we're addicted to our own passion, and so we keep saying *yes yes yes* to the chance to do more of it. Always more. Even when we're overloaded and we know it will be stressful, we take it on. I do this all the time and I'm betting that you do, too.

No is an extremely hard word. It's a two-letter word that everyone has a hard time using correctly.

In refining the method for Bluefishing, I've been forced to realize that while I understand and empathize with the people who want to say yes to everything, it's extremely destructive to let them continue down that path. It turns out, mastering the courage and ability to say no is a powerful element of Bluefishing. Learning when and when not to use the word *no* has far-reaching implications that go beyond just your work, and deep into the very heart of how you're spending your time on this planet.

You've got to realize that the more you bring into your life, the more you dilute what you're doing. It's just a simple fact that while humans can stretch and grow in remarkable ways, you shouldn't stretch yourself too thin all at once.

I've seen so many really good people go bankrupt and broke just because they don't know how to say no. I've seen companies fail because they say yes to every partnership, or yes to projects and people that don't line up with their own mission statement. You have to be able to say no. It might be that you have to say no to staff, to friends, to challenges, to projects, to new clients.

SAY NO TO VAMPIRES

No gives you the ability to fire people. You can fire anyone. Not just employees, but clients and customers too. You can even fire friends.

There are a lot of people in my life, the fantastic, good people that I like to be near just because they make me smile. There are people who are just good people to be with. I want to be clear about how simple this is. You drive a car because it makes sense. You wear an outfit because it makes you feel good. You have a friend because you enjoy each other. If you don't, why are you pretending to be friends?

Here's the dumbest thing in the world. You know you have a bad relationship with someone, but you tolerate it because, "I grew up with her," or "I work with them," or "She's my wife's best friend." You tolerate that relationship and you kid yourself that hey, it's just one bad relationship, it doesn't affect any of the others. That's where kidding yourself comes in, because the second that person's head pops up in your life, you go down. That person sucks something out of you, and the residue from that negativity lingers and hurts you for the rest of your day. How do you think you're going to start your next meeting? You don't go into it high. You don't go into it passionate. You don't go into it with generosity and love. You go into it with contempt or exhaustion.

You may really like the next person you're meeting with, but you're still stuck in a bad place. That person is going to pick up on it. He's going to think, "Oh, Steve's in a bit of a strange mood, he seems really off, is it something I've done?" That's not something you want someone feeling. Ever. If you're meeting with someone, you want to give them all of your energy and attention. You want them to feel good and confident around you, not back on their heels thinking they've done something wrong. The bad relationships you tolerate will start to poison all the other good relationships you have.

For example, I had to fire someone important to my team. She was our top salesperson. I knew the company would lose money for the next two months without her. Worse, I had known her for five years. I knew her birthdays; I knew her favorite foods, her favorite drink. In any working relationships, you open up to each other and you have a bond. But no matter what we did, every now and then, the bond would go sour, and then it continued to go sour. It was always an effort and a massive distraction to try to get it back on track. When there's more effort than good times, you know it's wrong.

Firing her wasn't easy, but I was immediately happier when she left. Not financially, but mentally. Removing that relationship added equity to my overall enthusiasm. I didn't have to get into a funked space by her texts or talk or negative energy knocking me off my game. Everyone on the team started to do better.

You have to be able to be powerful enough to say, "No. You're not helping my business or my life. In fact, you're a drain on both."

DON'T LET ANYBODY WASTE A MINUTE OF YOUR LIFE

There have been loads of people in my life I've been able to learn this from. Here's a great example: A mentor of mine and I were at a party. He was a salesman and he was very good at his job. Some other guy was really sucking up to him at this party. My friend took this clinger to one side to get a drink. The guy was beside himself because he was personally getting a drink from this great salesman. My friend bought him a drink and said, quite kindly, "Look, I don't mean you any disrespect, but I can assure you that there is something different between our characters that isn't going to work out well. I mean you no disrespect, but we're never going to be friends."

I stood there next to them, and I thought, "Holy shit!" This was a whole new level. My friend said to the guy, "So, please. This event is a great opportunity for you to go talk to someone who can really be good for you and your network, but I don't want you to waste your energy here tonight with me." I thought to myself, "Wow! What a kick in the nuts!" But my friend did it with such sincerity, he had his hand on the guy's shoulder, and then he said, "That guy over there, he's a good person for you to chat with, you know?" Later on that night, the first guy came back over to my friend and said, "Thanks. I get it." And my friend just said, "You're welcome." There was sincere respect going both ways.

I was in my twenties at the time thinking dumb things like "I'm going to live forever, I'm the shit, I'm the man." I remember my friend turning around and saying, "Don't let anybody waste a minute of your life. You can't get it back."

AUDIT YOUR INNER CIRCLE

Write down all the people in your life. Remember when you did a self-audit back in Chapter 10, so you could figure out where your personal strengths and weaknesses were? This is the next step. This is an audit of your circle. It's like a spring cleaning of the people who have had the most impact on your life. You can do it by drawing concentric circles, starting with the small one in the middle and thinking, "Who's closest to me? Okay, who's next closest?" You can work that audit from the inside out, from family, friends, vendors, partners, clients, customer—all the way out to the outer circles. No matter how far they are on that outer circle, they're still in your zone. They're still in your solar system. They still have an impact.

Once you do your audit, consider it objectively. Circle the good, scratch out the bad, ignore the indifferent. It's not hard on paper. We know who to cut when we do an analysis.

When you need to cut someone from your business operations, don't just think about what they're contributing to the bottom line. Think about whether they lift you up, brighten the office, help your team get things done. Are they totally aligned with what you are all trying to do, and are they making your business something you enjoy spending years of your life on? If they're not, you know what to do.

When it comes to a personal level, those people probably have more influence on your life than the businesspeople. In business if I say I want a new accountant, I find one. I can't just one day say I want a new wife, that's for sure, not without seismic consequences. (For some, of course, this might just be the thing to do. Some changes are little. Others are very, very big.) The people in our families are often the ones closest to us, and sadly they can have the most power to do the most harm. They're quite often the ones that you have to turn around and go, "Look, you've got your own life. I've got mine. When you fall down or you're in need, yes, as blood, I'll be there. As friends, though, this doesn't work. It doesn't work for me, it doesn't work for you. We shouldn't spend the energy on trying to do something that doesn't work." In the end, you'll find that if you're spending so much of your life trying to make something good that isn't, by doing so you are making many other things in your life bad.

Listen, saying no in a big way to someone close to you is really painful, no question. No one said this was easy. We did not start this chapter saying, "Hey, here's an easy fix." This is going deep, and it's painful, but this is a critical element of truly mastering Bluefishing. Once you've stood on your own two feet and said no to someone, you'll feel freer and lighter in ways you never imagined.

You see, it's nobody else's life. It's yours and yours alone. How you react to the assholes or the mismatches in your life isn't going to give you extra years of living. It's not going to give you any extra dollars either. You've got a certain amount of time on this green grass and you need to use it well and make beautiful things happen.

That's the power of no. It helps you cut the fat and focus on the meat. Get used to it, try it in small steps until it becomes a habit, and it'll become a very, very strong resource to make sure you don't waste time doing stuff that doesn't benefit you and the things you're trying to get done in your life.

SECRETS FROM
THE BLUEFISHING PLAYBOOK

★ Master the courage to say no: Remember the more you bring into your life, the more you dilute what you can do well.

★ Audit your inner circle: *No* gives you the ability to fire the vampires. You can fire customers. You can even fire friends. Determine who adds energy to your time and who sucks it out.

TWELVE

THE ART OF DELEGATION

There's something that happens to anyone who starts to become more confident and competent in what they do. As soon as they achieve a little bit of success, they want more. More success, more accolades, more achievement. That jeopardizes their ability to say no and they end up taking on absolutely everything. We already talked about how, especially for entrepreneurs, this can be one of our most devastating traits. What's worse is that, once we take something on, we often try to do every single element of it ourselves.

The trouble with achievers or entrepreneurs is that we try to hold onto the entire project ourselves and we basically implode the whole damn thing. (I'm not sure why we do this. Because we care so much? Because we're control freaks? Because we're so good at getting things done on our own?) We squeeze the project so hard that no one else can get to it, nobody gets to run with it, and we suffocate it completely. Then, of course, we're left with depression because there's no one to blame other than ourselves.

LEARN TO LEAD THE ORCHESTRA

There needs to be a time when you can walk into a project, and say, "Look, there's a difference between being able to do everything and doing everything."

I believe that there is 5 percent within each of us that is just wildly and totally unique—it's the thing you can do that no one else can do. It's important to know what your 5 percent is. This lets you know where you're strongest and what you're the best at. Then carve out the part of your project that perfectly matches your specific and unique skills. Let the other 95 percent of the project get done by other people. That's when you become an orchestra conductor. You can recognize what needs to be done and you just orchestrate it, so that you can lead your team in an amazing symphony. When you're able to do that, you're also able to scale. You can scale your business to new heights, while also scaling your capacity for knocking down walls and getting things done in all aspects of your life.

Let's say that you've got fifteen people working for you. Your real opportunity for growth lies in answering this: How much do I let people run with things on their own, and how much do I rope them back in? How much do I oversee, and how much do I let them make mistakes?

First, you *oversee* everything. You don't get to take your eye off the ball ever, even if other people are doing 95 percent of the work. It's up to you to keep the overall health of the project in front of you at all times. This method isn't meant to let you slack off, but rather, to set you up with a way to let other people run with most of the tasks, so you can run with the part that you're best at. You have to grow by delegating responsibility, if you want to have any chance at scaling and growing your business. If you try to do it all yourself, you and your company will never grow and, as I said before, you'll end up suffocating the whole thing. Remember, if you're not growing, you're dying.

Then look at the most important part of your project. You want to make sure that whatever is critical, whatever can hurt you or hurt the business, is looked after by those nearest and dearest to you. Your most trusted colleagues, the ones you chat with all the time, the people whose 5 percent you already know.

For a critical element of a project, sometimes I will go to two different people and give them the same task. That helps me discover where their unique 5 percent is, while at the same time doubling my chances of having a successful result delivered to me. All you want is to find a whole bunch of people with unique abilities, all with their own 5 percent traits or skills that no one else can do. That's how you build up an irreplaceable team. A dream team.

Once you know that the most important pieces of your project are in good hands, take another look at the big picture and say, "Okay, this project has ten legs. Which of those legs can I cut off without it impacting the rest of the company?" Those are the ones that carry the least risk. Objectively try to match people up with the tasks at hand. Assign them things that match *their* 5 percent, their best elements. Give each of them the ability to obsess over their one part of the project. Delegate those, outsource them, and let them run. Don't try to herd too much.

I use outsourcing a lot. It may cost you twenty-five hundred dollars, or it may cost you ten dollars. For example, I've got a guy who edits my videos, makes the color pop a little bit, fine tunes the sound, puts the before and after footage on there with my logo, and he charges me ten dollars. Of course, I had to go through a lot of cost and about six video guys before I found him. Now, every time I do a video, I send it to him right away. He's based in England. He fixes it up and I get it back the following day.

YOU CAN ONLY GROW BY GIVING OTHER PEOPLE RESPONSIBILITY

You've got to grow, and you can only grow by giving other people responsibility. People will fuck up, people will let you down, sure enough. But part of that process helps you discover where their strengths and weaknesses are. When you find a weakness, note it. Either get them to work on improving it, or else don't let them do anything with responsibility in that area. You don't send a shy math genius to charm clients at a nightclub. Then, if you've tried and someone just doesn't have the 5 percent you need, or they have too many weaknesses to make them worth it (and definitely if they're a time vampire), get someone else.

GIVE PEOPLE ENOUGH ROPE TO CLIMB OR HANG THEMSELVES

Here's a secret that only achiever types who have been there will understand. Controlling everything is very lonely, and having only yourself to blame when it bombs feels terrible. If you can learn to delegate your projects to capable people, and if you put effort into making sure each task matches up with the right person, you're going to see this team rising up around you. It doesn't necessarily have to be a full-time, salaried, 401k kind of team. I mean that it's a crew of people who you know are good at what they do, who can get shit done, and who free you up to focus on being the conductor instead of going crazy trying to play every instrument in the pit. With a crew like that, the growth that you and your business will experience is terrific. Not only will you get exponentially more done: You also won't be alone anymore.

GAIN THE EXTRA TIME TO DO WHAT'S GOOD

Here's a different way to look at the art of delegation and the freedom it can bring you.

I mentioned earlier that my biggest fear is being exactly where I was last week, last month, just stuck in a standstill. So I try to incorporate different things into my life every now and then that will challenge an emotion or elicit a reaction from either myself or others. I can see how it works (or not) and ask, "Do I like that? Do you?" And, of course, I don't always get it right the first time. To be honest, there are more times I get it wrong than right but, like investing in a start-up company, when you get it right, you get it fucking-A right. That's the beauty of investing in yourself.

One of the things I tried was hiring a personal chef. I

know, that might sound like an irrelevant, bogus, rich-guy example, but it's not. Come on people, I was a bricklayer, remember? And stick with me, because this experiment wound up paying for itself in spades.

I knew someone who was making meals for a local family. I spoke with him and asked him to make and deliver all of my dinner meals from Monday to Friday. Sometimes, you get so busy and have no time to prepare healthy, home-cooked food. "I'm hungry, what's for dinner? Let's get Chinese! Let's get pizza!" People typically eat poorly when they're in a hurry. Fast-food is convenient but not great on the waistline. I wanted to see if there was a way of having that convenience and saying, "I want to be healthy. I like paleo, I like basic, I like chicken, vegetables, rice. Can you look after me?"

We agreed that the chef would do dinner and dessert and get me eating better. We tried it for a month, and what I ended up receiving was something I didn't expect. I ended up receiving two hours to four hours a day. Now, I can make you slimmer. I can make you fitter, I can make you more interesting; I can help make you wealthier. What I can't get you is more hours in a day. But I was able to get two to four hours a day by having a chef. This extra time was a byproduct of this experiment, and it absolutely stunned the shit out of me.

You see, my wife works with me in the office, and many times one of us has to break away from something important to run down to the grocery store to get the dinner for us and the kids. It's usually about ten o'clock in the morning when this thought crosses her mind: "What should we have for dinner tonight?" Once we start that conversation, like it or not, what we are doing is taking our eye off the ball.

When you're doing something and you look down, you slow down. When you take your eye off whatever you're doing, you lose something. It takes thirty to forty minutes to get back up to speed with the task you were working on before you stepped away.

When we got this chef, we no longer had that ten o'clock question about what do for or dinner, or the five o'clock phone call, "Oh, I've got to start thinking of something for the kids," and then later at home, "I've got to start getting some dinner ready." Those interruptions, small though they might seem, completely ended during this experiment. The dinner turned up at five-thirty with heating instructions. We followed the instructions and, twenty minutes later, we were eating. Also, we had barely any dirty dishes to do.

I was saving so much time during the day, and my wife was also saving time, so collectively we saved two to four hours to get things done. Two people now had more time. I found other benefits from it, like having more time to play with the kids. It's really wonderful when, at five, you don't have to start rushing around thinking, "What am I gonna feed the kids tonight?" Instead you can sit down and help them with their homework, or have a chat, or play a game. You gain the extra time to do what's good.

EFFICIENCY TRANSLATES TO TIME SAVED

You can tell I think about time a lot these days.

How often do you hear this as a business pitch: "If you buy this product, it's going to save you hours a day!" You hear this about everything from speed workout machines to personal virtual assistants, productivity hacks, delivery services, and more, like my chef example. You'll read business blogs and lifestyle or start-up books (and even this one) that beg you not to waste a single minute of the time you get on this green Earth. You probably hear it quite a bit.

When people ask me where to invest, like I'm a shark on *Shark Tank*, I say that smart money is going toward anything time-saving. So, my two cents: Anything that saves you time, that's what you want to piggyback on right now, that's what you want to develop. Anything that can give us back a little time to spend with our families, make the most out of our days, get more work done, that's where the smart money is. Efficiency and timesaving.

Here's an example. People initially started taking Uber cars because they knew the ride would be there when they wanted it, and they wouldn't have to go stand in the rain waiting for a taxi to drive by. They fell in love with the service when they realized they could easily Uber instead of driving their own cars and looking for parking, when they noticed that they could check their email and get work done from the back seat. Uber maximized their work time. So hard-working business people became a core constituency for Uber.

The food industry is also headed for a big shakeup. I've been watching delivery services for a while. I think this is because we have more working millennials now. You know how it is when you're young. You work, you go out afterward with your friends, and by the time you get home, you barely have time to sleep, much less cook. So there are a lot of food companies popping up that deliver good, healthy food, and save people so much time. That time-saving function is why I think food is a big industry that's interesting to watch.

You can't really reinvent the mouse trap, but if you're

looking for a great idea to build out or invest in, look for something that's going to catch a mouse a little more efficiently. Because we can all learn how to make more money. But not a single person on Earth knows how to make more time.

THE SMALL STUFF GNAWS
AT THE BIG PICTURE

The real art of delegation, Bluefish style, is actually about learning how to put time into what matters. This means learning how *not to spend time on things that slow you down.*

Start small. Look at all areas of your life and your work habits. Ask yourself, "What are the moments of my day that aggravate me?" Is there a way to change small stuff to gain better focus without trying to reinvent the wheel? Look at the ways during the day you can save time by cutting out an element of stress.

Can you hire a virtual assistant to do small things for you, like research a new dentist for the kids? Or call the water company for you to schedule a water audit, so that you can cut down on your monthly bill during a drought? Can you subscribe to monthly deliveries of dog food, or diapers, or beer, so you don't have to run to the store late at night when you run out? What are the small things you can outsource or schedule or hack so that you don't take your eye off the bigger stuff. There are tons of resources and start-ups out there empowering this way of thinking. Take thirty minutes to identify your recurring stressors, and I bet there's a solution waiting for you.

Allowing little stressors to bounce around in our daily lives is more detrimental than we're aware of. They chip away at our time and energy, one by one. Allow enough of these to run free in your life, and the effect is slowly but surely cumulative, with a dark cloud constantly overhead.

SECRETS FROM
THE BLUEFISHING PLAYBOOK

*   There's a difference between being able to do everything and *doing* everything. You can only grow by giving other people responsibility. That's the only way you and your business will ever manage to scale.
*   It's About Time—The real art of delegation, Bluefish style, is actually about learning how to put time into what matters. This means learning how not to spend time on things that slow you down.

THIRTEEN

WHAT MAKES A BRAND GREAT?

Founders and CEOs always ask me: "How can I make my company into a great brand?

My first answer is to forget the word *great*. Yes, you want to do something that's phenomenal, you want to make big change in the world and you want your business to be wildly successful. But *great* is not a goal that you can see. So, if you want to make your business great, begin with something else. First, work to make it better than it was yesterday, and constantly strive to make it better, day over day, month over month. It's a progression, an evolution.

When we were first building Bluefish into a company, we were called lots of things. We were called a concierge service, we were called party promoters, but we never adopted those names. We never wanted to play with that tribe because it didn't resonate with us, and a business just about travel and partying felt limiting compared to the massive life events and happiness we knew we could make happen for people.

A tagline is usually your elevator pitch as to what you do. Tension headache? Take Advil. That tagline goes underneath your brand name to explain quickly what you do. BMW, "the ultimate driving machine" and "we only make one thing." They've got their taglines. We could have very easily defined Bluefish as "the best party in the world." But didn't want to adopt that tagline because what we wanted to do, once we knew where we were heading, was something different. I'm not building a travel agency. I'm not building a wish-fulfillment center. I'm building a brand. Because companies don't establish communities. Brands do.

HOW DO YOU ESTABLISH A PRESTIGE BRAND?

Prestige can be described in one word: Desire. If you *desire* something, then to you it is something prestigious, it is luxurious. There's no reason behind it. There's no *reason* on Earth to buy a forty-five-thousand-dollar watch. There's no reason to buy a car that can do over two hundred miles per hour. There's no reason behind any of those things, other than lust and desire. And that's what makes them luxurious. There's no reason behind a prestige brand.

Once you wrap your head around that, you start to understand that building a prestige brand is not about calling out the logical features and benefits of the thing you're selling, but about whipping up an emotional frenzy for it within a specific community.

Compare a Hyundai with an Audi. You have the same reliability, warranty, all that. But at the end of the day, you *desire* the Audi, not the Hyundai, and that's what propels it from being a brand to a luxury brand, a prestige brand.

The first thing you've got to do is get others to comment on your brand. If you say that your product is great, that's just selling. But if someone else says you've got something good, it's a recommendation, and others want in. People always want what other people want.

FORBES AND THE "COOL GUY" ARTICLE

In April, 2016 *Forbes* magazine wrote a piece about me, Steve Sims. Not about my company, Bluefish. The gist of the article was laughably simple: "Cool guy." That was it. I was just doing what I'd been doing for twenty years. There wasn't any news in the article, nothing earth shattering. But that comment in *Forbes* did more than I could have done with a million dollars of my own "prestige" branding. It was seven pages of ink that I couldn't have bought for any amount.

Everyone I had ever known started reaching out wanting to do business with me. Now that *Forbes* told them what I've been telling them for years, people wanted in. What brands need to do—both personal and business brands—is ask other people to validate the truth. What do you think my company stands for? What do you think our message is? Because their perception, what they see, that's the truth about your brand. Once you've figured out how people see your brand, and it resonates with who you are and what you're building, then you can take a look at positioning your products and services and partnerships. But the first get people to say the right things about you.

FOCUS ON YOUR STRENGTHS AND IGNORE YOUR WEAKNESSES

Or you end up with a lot of really strong weaknesses. Prestige brands don't focus on delivering *everything*. They usually go deep on delivering one thing really well. Even more important, they don't set out to make sales. A sale is a transaction. Instead, they set out from the very beginning to create an experience for someone. An experience is something you will tell a friend about.

When you go to a Rolex store, you don't go up to an ATM watch machine, push a button, it drops a Rolex, and you walk out the door. Yes, you can buy one online, but most people buy that first luxury watch by walking into the store, having the salesman talk to them, browsing through glittering options and feeling the experience of that. "I'm the kind of person who belongs in here and can afford a watch like this." Is that logical? Rational? Efficient? Not even close. But you're there for the desire of the thing. You're there for the experience.

A writer friend loves Mont Blanc pens. He knows a Mont Blanc is just a pen, but to him it holds a meaning and a benchmark of achievement after struggling for so many years. Whenever he sells a new book to a fancy publisher, he buys another of these brand name pens. You see, *prestige* is in his head. He knows he could buy a perfectly functional pen from Staples. He laughs and says he could buy a lifetime supply of pens from an office supply store that would be cheaper than one Mont Blanc. But that brand hooked his desire.

SECRETS FROM
THE BLUEFISHING PLAYBOOK

★ *Great* is not a goal you can see. If you want to make your business great, first work to make it better than it was yesterday,

★ Get the right people to say the right things about you. That's marketing in a nutshell.

FOURTEEN

THE ART OF
SPEAKING HUMAN

J ust fifteen years ago, the world was a different planet. We didn't have iPhones, texting, selfies, Facebook, Snapchat, Twitter. I like social technology. It is, in many aspects, a brilliant improvement for society that enhances many things. But there's something people keep saying that I can't agree with. They say, "Technology is allowing us to communicate better."

It's not. It's diluting communication and allowing us to shield ourselves from each other.

I remember my mom giving me a grocery list when I was a kid. I'd have to trundle down to the store and pick it all up. An entire week's worth. Then she'd go down on Saturday and settle up on the bill. You were your word. It was as simple as that. If you said you were going to do something, you were going to do it. And because this was your village, your community, and you'd see that person again next week, you always did it.

There are some great community structures online, to be sure. I'm thinking of Reddit. I'm thinking about how when someone is popular on Instagram and does it right, their fans always defend them from the trolls in the comments section.

But in business? That's harder. Most businesses use social technology to yell their message, as often as possible. It's a turkey shoot, and they hope they hit someone. That's their idea of marketing.

And what about their idea of engagement? Since business is majorly run on e-commerce these days, it's almost impossible to have a village-based relationship. I buy toilet paper from Amazon. I'm a customer. I'm not part of Amazon's community. There isn't one, because there's no relationship. I'm a transaction.

The best they can offer might be so-called live chat. You don't know who you're speaking with at any point. It could be a twelve-year-old in Malaysia, for all you know. The two of you are strangers having a forgettable exchange.

Businesses measure engagement in numbers, like how long someone stayed on their website, or how many sales were made, or how many Likes a Facebook post got. I say there's nothing engaged about that.

When you tweet at someone, text someone, you're not communicating with them, you're shooting a message at them. You could say, "Dinner tonight?" That's not the same as reaching out on the phone, or even videoing ten seconds of yourself and saying: "Hey, friend! What are you up to tonight? I've been working too hard and want to take a break and see you, can we grab a bite?" It's more enticing when you actually get the voice. We are physical, biological beings who run fully on our senses of sight, smell, hearing, taste, and touch. Sending a tweet to someone doesn't resonate with any of those senses. We are dulling our senses if this is how we communicate for most of our day.

The phone has its own problems, as phone calls are becoming incredibly intrusive. You're busy writing, you're responding to emails, you're building up a proposal, you're designing the website, you're in your zone where your brain is flowing and feeling good and focused. And all of a sudden, a fire alarm goes off in the form of a phone call. There's not a single person on earth who doesn't feel annoyance as their first blink response to a ringing phone when they were busy doing something else.

What if, instead, you try this: Take a little selfie video and text it to the person you need to chat with. For example, I'd say, "Hey, mate, I'm in my garage working on my bike, I'm in my zone. Can I give you a call in a few minutes? I really want to catch up with you." Now there's so much more going on. The person gets to hear your voice, see the twinkle in your eye, see a cool little backdrop. They have visuals, audio, they can sense my passion; they can see, feel, and hear. There are more senses being used in that message.

WHAT MAKES BUSINESS PERSONAL?

I believe quite simply that the way to hack this technology-driven communication problem, especially in business, is that you must make what you stand for personally available to the consumer. There is nothing more important in business now than Bluefishing. And Bluefishing is as simple as this: It's the art of speaking human.

Everything you do in business, everything *you* do in business, has to resonate with what the business is. You've got to take a personal approach with your vendors; the way you treat your vendors, the way you treat your staff, the way you treat those around you will come through in your business. You shouldn't try to hide behind the old Sun Tzu Japanese business philosophy, "It's only business." It's not only business. You can't afford to be only business now. We're not looking for cold transaction services. Humans aren't looking for efficiencies and sterility. We're looking to relate, we're looking to join a pack, and we're looking to emulate people. So, you've got to stand up on what you've built and say, "Look, this is what I built, because this is what I care about, this is what I do, this is who I am."

NEVER MIND THE STRANGERS

The key to business in this era is not having as many customers as possible. Believe it or not, it's not clients. It's not likes, it's not followers. It's building a village connection around the thing you do. A community. A community is solid, loyal, loving, it looks after each other, spreads the word, cares.

Here's where the advantage is. This is when it gets beautiful, when you take the time to actually reach out to the people in your community in a way that they can sense, listen, and feel.

Find out who your inner circle is, the people who really like what you're making, and focus on them. Get *ugly* (remember, that means raw, authentic, weird, funny) with them. Try to engage them in a way that actually engages their senses (not just their clicking or swiping finger). Let them see who you are and why you're spending so much time, out of your very short time on this green earth, working on something that you think would be good for them.

You can't concentrate on your friends when you're giving all your time to strangers.

There's a world of noise out there. If you let technology set the rules for your communication, and if you hide behind emails and automated drip campaigns and scheduled Facebook posts, no one will even hear you.

You have to use technology to put your presence forward, rather than relying on simple text and shortcut grammar to get your message across. That leaves us unmoved, even if we can't put our finger on the emptiness.

If you go back to the basics: writing letters, sending postcards, sending videos, using the phone to phone people, creating events and moments for your community, taking the time to connect one person to another with a clap on the shoulder and a handshake, you get to engage all the senses. You get to project *you*. And everyone wants to work with unique, individual people. As I said before, you're already unique and individual from birth. Now, they get to see it.

SECRETS FROM
THE BLUEFISHING PLAYBOOK

★ You can't concentrate on your friends when you're giving all your time to strangers.

★ Don't let technology set the rules for your communication. If you hide behind emails and tweets, no one will ever hear you.

FIFTEEN

GIVE THEM A REASON TO BELIEVE

A friend of mine recently asked me to give a talk for his club. It was a seminar for independent financial advisers, mainly accountants and stock brokers, none of your big price-tag Wall Street hotshots. Mostly, conservative older men who had been doing the same job for a long time. It was held at an airport hotel on the outskirts of San Francisco; not a lot of glitz and glamor there.

I turned up in my usual black shirt, jeans and leather jacket, walked into the thing, looked around and immediately thought, "Oh, God. I'm in for it." On stage, there was a gentleman talking about 'new actuary calculative software.' Just *looking* at his slide show, I thought to myself, "I'm definitely not the right guy for this crowd."

Still, I was determined to do my best. I probably had

thirty people in my session. It was just us in a crowded, tiny room in the hotel. Very low energy at the start.

I went through the usual kind of introduction about what I do. The usual, "Hey, if you ever wanted to meet your favorite actor, or do something you never dreamed was possible, this is how I do this and this." I could see their eyes glazing over pretty quickly. They weren't here for that. I needed to switch gears and get smarter about what they were into, so I started chatting with them. The first thing that came up was that they had spent four grand to be at this event.

"That's good," I said. "Obviously you care about investing in yourself, because you want professional growth, and you want to keep getting better at what you do." I saw nods go around the room. So, I continued, "Okay, so how many of your clients know you're here today?" No one raised their hand. None of their clients knew that they were there. In their view, they didn't want their clients to know that they were out of the office right now. This really caught me by surprise. I decided to ax the prepared speech and just talk to these people.

THE ROI ON YOU

I said, "Let me get this right. These people need you. They all employ you to look after their money, make them more money, make sure it's protected for their retirement or in case of death. They trust you to look after that. Right?" They were all nodding. I kept on. "Shouldn't they know that you invest not only in the market, but you also invest in yourselves? And therefore the ROI on you is constantly growing. And when the ROI on you grows, their money and opportunity grows too. Today, you are smarter than you were yesterday, and you'll be smarter tomorrow when this whole three-day seminar finishes . . . ." I paused.

Then, I said, "And you couldn't give your clients the courtesy to let them know that you're here, growing, and constantly raising the bar on your success and that, by doing so, you're directly benefiting their success too?

The room was still. They were completely dumb-founded by that concept. None of them had even thought to reach out to their people and say, "Hey, I respect the relationship that we have, but it's not good enough for me. I want to be better. I'm going to be away for the next three days because I am going to a convention to get even better for you." I asked them, "Wouldn't that make your clients want to stay with you more than ever? Wouldn't that give them a reason to believe in you?"

This question was completely strange to them. It got me thinking that if we care about the quality of our relationships with our clients, our family, our friends, we should let them know about the good things we are doing to grow, to get better. Not with Facebook pictures of phony crap. Not, "Hey, look at me, I'm in a fancy restaurant, I'm drinking a weird drink, I'm on a plane, look at my Tesla." Instead, let them know that you want to grow. Everything is evolution, everything around us is moving at exponential speed. I asked the crowd, "Shouldn't the people in your circle know that you are also working hard to grow at that same rate?"

Finally, I started to win these guys over. "Let's be honest," I continued, "don't you usually communicate with your clients only when there's a problem? Don't you wish you had a reason to send them a note with good news, something to impress them? In business you're reactive or you're proactive. Well, you're here, so I think you're proactive and that you want to do more for your clients.

Next, I asked them, "Put your hands up; who among you has gotten every cent and business possible from your clients?" And, of course, no hands went up. I said, "So you're missing out on making the most of existing business and also on recruiting new business. You haven't told your people that you're here. They may not know that you now specialize in an actuary analysis program, and they might have a friend who needs just that."

How can you reach your clients to build trust and loyalty? Email blasts to everyone? For every hundred emails you send out, you would be damn lucky if five people open and read them. What do you think is better, that, or to have someone with credibility at a party telling five people that you're the magical gold dust they need. That's better marketing than sending twenty thousand emails. "So," I asked the group, "Shouldn't you be doing something different from relying on your email campaigns for so-called communication?"

IF COMMUNICATION ISN'T PERSONAL, IT'S NOT COMMUNICATION

You need to take the time to get to know your clients. Send them something that they like. Let's say you've got a client who is traveling to Italy next month. Why don't you run to your bookstore, and bookstores need help, so go into any bookstore, which always has a discount area where they're trying to offload books. Usually the big books with all the pretty pictures are in those discount areas. The client's going to Italy, so get him an Italian cookbook and send it over with a nice note tucked away inside. Or a good novel and coloring books to keep them and their kids busy on the plane. Or how about one of those travel plugs for the right country. How many times do people travel, even in this massively technology-driven time, and go, "Crap, I've got my hair dryer, I've got my iPhone, I've got my computer. But I don't have the travel plug again!' So, buy a travel plug.

Remember, it's about being "ugly" and raw and real and personal. Not about polish and prescriptive perfection.

I gave everyone in the room homework. "Tonight," I said, "When you're up in your room, grab the box of hotel stationery and write to five of your clients. Say, "I'm just dropping you a little note. I'm on a three-day seminar soaking up new knowledge of this thing, and I'm going to reach out to you in the next couple of weeks to let you know how we can apply what I'm learning to your account." That doesn't cost you any more than the stamp.

Speaking of stamps, and taking a quick detour for a second: How about when your client's baby is born, and they send you a cute picture and you have no idea as to what to send them to say congrats? Here's an idea: Get a book of stamps made out of that baby picture and send it back to them so they can tell all their friends that someone new and special is in the family.

Now, remember, I might have been winning the guys in that hotel room over, but I'm still in a crowd of financial advisers, people who count money for a living. So at one point, one guy shouts out (and there's always one in any room), "Yeah, it's very easy to be impressive when someone is giving you two million dollars to make something big happen in Italy." He continued, "I've got a client who loves diamonds and rings. If I want to look after him and show him I care, I've gotta buy a Cartier ring?"

HOW MUCH DOES IT COST TO LISTEN?

The best things in the world are small prices: twenty, fifty, way under one hundred dollars. When there's a birthday coming up in my family, we give everyone in the house twenty-five dollars. If I tell them they can't spend more than that each, sometimes they clump together because they need forty dollars to pull it off. When you start working at it like that, you get some of the coolest things in the world.

So, I said to the skeptical guy, "Your client who collects those Cartier rings, you could send him a book on Cartier. You could phone a jeweler and get him a private course on how to tell the grade of the diamond. You could get a high-end cleaning kit for him. Or a new loupe to look at the diamonds he already has. All of these things enhance what he's already collecting."

If the guy collects artwork, don't try to buy him a piece

of artwork, buy him something that exemplifies and enhances his pleasure of that artwork. If a client loves baseball, don't get him expensive tickets to the Series; send him a baseball for his kid, with a note rubber-banded around it.

Small gifts engage people. They're opening up a package. The anticipation is building. They hear the ripping paper. Who hears an email? So, they open the gift, say it's a book, they open the book, and there's a Sharpie hand-written note in there from you. "Just thought I'd give you a quick read for the weekend and thought you'd like this one. All the best."

It takes longer to open a package than it takes to open any email you've ever sent them. That book may end up in the bin three seconds later, but it doesn't matter. Your point has come across, and they will, nine times out of ten reach out to you and just say, 'Hey, thanks!'

My airport hotel crowd listening to all these ideas went from stiff suits to literally standing up and jumping around, as they were asking questions and sharing ideas for things they could try out with their clients.

The whole point is that the cost of the thing itself is irrelevant. What you're doing is showing that you totally listen to your client and have a dedicated, one-on-one relationship with him or her. Personalization of communication is so easy to do and has such a huge impact. It amplifies the fact that you care, it shows that you're listening, and it takes you from being transactional to actually building up a community.

SECRETS FROM
THE BLUEFISHING PLAYBOOK

* If communication isn't personal, it's not communication.
* Have someone with credibility at a party telling five people that you are the magical gold dust they need. That's better marketing than sending out twenty thousand emails.

SIXTEEN

SPONGE IT UP

I recently got one of those blast-from-the-past phone calls from a guy I've known since we were fourteen. He was never my best buddy, but he was one of the crew back then. One of those guys that you know everything about; you know what he drinks, you know about his parents, you know the girls he's slept with, you know all that kind of stuff, but he's never your first choice to call and check in with when you have a free minute. I hadn't heard from him in decades.

Then he read that article about me in *Forbes* and reached out. We started chatting by text message, then I said, "My fingers are getting tired, just hit Skype and I'll carry on working and we'll chat and see each other at the same time." In a few minutes, I had him on Skype chatting, and I've never felt someone so unsure, so unconfident. But he *was* confident about all his excuses for why he hadn't done anything with his life. People are always very confident to give you a reason why they can't do something, and not at all confident to give you a reason why they can.

He said he was impressed that I was doing so well. "It's because you're smart," he said. "Smarter than me, and you've pulled it off."

I said, "You're kidding me, man? I'm no smarter now than when I was laying bricks! And I was crap at that! Yes, I've found things out, I've discovered what works, what doesn't work, and I've learned a lot. But I'm still the same guy. I'm not some kind of intellect now."

His end of the connection was silent. I ventured to him, "Mate, the only difference between you and me is that I was willing to get into uncomfortable situations. I was willing to look dumb, to be among people that I knew were far more intelligent than me, so that I could learn. There's no reason to get into a room with people stupider than you.

"You've got to realize you're an idiot," I said.

He said, "Yeah, I do." He was totally deflated. I could hear it and see it.

I said, "No, no, no, I'm not calling you an idiot. You know I mean it in another way. You have to recognize that you're an idiot at something, and be comfortable with your status of not-knowing, so that you can take that self-knowledge, walk into a room and say to yourself, 'Hey, I'm an idiot right now, but I'm here to get just one percent smarter.'

"Go in there open-armed, open-brained, open-headed, shut up, and let it come in. Sit like a sponge in a room full of water and just soak it all in. That's what you've got to do. You've literally got to suck it up. As soon as you get smart at that thing, or you start to think you're getting smarter, quick, get into another room where you're an idiot again."

I continued to tell this old buddy of mine looking for advice, "You've got to be willing to do that. Get into uncomfortable situations."

GET ON YOUR BOOTS AND GO

Remember, if you stretch an elastic band five times, then let it go, it will never go back to the same small size it originally was. That's what you've got to do with your mentality. If you keep stretching yourself, as a practice and as a habit, your capacity for things will grow. You'll never shrink back to where you started. Your ability will just keep getting bigger.

People like being in a rut. People like knowing what they know, and being ignorant of what they don't know.

People complain about it, but they're comfortable there. As I said, they're confident giving excuses for why they can't do something. If you want to do something, don't give yourself a single excuse up front. You can come up with excuses afterward for why it didn't work, if you really need a defense mechanism. But don't do that before you even started. Just go and do it. I mentioned paralysis by analysis earlier. While people are thinking about things and planning it to death, I've already put my shoes on and gone and done it.

The Bluefishing creed is move, act, do, go. Action is everything. Learn what you don't know, then try again.

I've done this so many times. I've opened doors that I shouldn't have been able to. I've gone into rooms I shouldn't have had access to. I've gone into lectures that I was ill-equipped to be in. I've sat in meetings where I didn't know my head from my arsehole, but you know, every time I've stretched myself, I've grown. I haven't shrunk. Do this enough, and you'll discover that the very meeting you snuck into a month ago, you're now leading.

I joke that there should be an Olympics for excuses. There are so many people who are comfortable giving themselves reasons to fail. They specialize in it. These people don't wind up doing anything at all, in most aspects of their life. When you ask them point blank, "Why didn't you do that?" They're lightning fast at giving you reasons why they couldn't or didn't try to do something. They put so much mental and emotional effort into the excuse, it has to be exhausting. It almost seems easier to just be willing to get up, do it, risk it, and soak it all in.

THE TWIN DEVILS OF FEAR
AND EMBARRASSMENT

I believe there are two things that cause this kind of behavior. It's not that you're stupid or lazy or a bad person. It's this: Fear and embarrassment. People don't like embarrassment; people don't like to be laughed at. At school when they're laughed at, it's a bad thing. To get into an environment where they're not comfortable, they stand the risk of being laughed at. Embarrassment holds so many people back and keeps them in their rut, instead of letting them venture a single step out of their safe comfort zone. They'd rather be where they are and know where they are, than actually risk it and grow.

And then there's fear. Fear of embarrassment, but even more than that. People are actually scared of growth. "What if I do get that promotion? What if I do close that deal, investment, partnership, whatever. I'll be more responsible. I'll be on a higher wire. More eyes on me." So much pressure. They're so frightened of it actually happening that they would rather be stationary, with their head in the sand, because at least it's a known routine.

I'm frightened of being exactly where I was two months ago. Some people might say, "Okay, I don't want to be in the exact same job or financial position in twelve months." They give themselves that much time. Me, I don't want to be in the same situation that I was in last month. That may have been a phenomenal situation. I don't want to be there again though. I don't want my finances to be the same. I don't want my business plateauing on the same level. I don't want to be involved in the same exact stuff I was a month, two months, three months ago. I want to grow. I want to go outward. I want to expand. My fear is being in the same place—static. That's not the nature of reality. The world's constantly changing. You're out of sync if you're not changing.

SOAK UP JUST 1 PERCENT MORE THAN YOU KNEW YESTERDAY

To take charge of your growth, Bluefish style, you have to get into your sponge mentality. First, think about it this way: It's actually very easy to be a sponge. No one is expecting you to be the smartest person in the room or to put on a show or lead or change minds. Not if you walk in and say, "Hey, I'm new to this, but I'm committed to growing and I want to learn one percent more about this today. Think you can help me do that for the next hour?" Where's the pressure in that? You get to just open your brain and receive. You get to catch. That's way easier than throwing.

The next part of taking charge of your growth, Bluefish style, is in the *action*. You can't soak something in if you're sitting in the same room, alone, day in and day out. You have to find things to soak up, people to learn from, experiences to extract learning from. You've got to get out there, put yourself out there. You have to shut down those voices in your head (and I promise they're only in your head) saying, "You can't do this, you can't do that." In other words, whenever you take a risk, you're all the time going to learn something that you'll walk away with. Guaranteed growth. You've got to be prepared to lie down, be vulnerable (which won't kill you, believe me) and soak it up.

I completely get that it sounds hard and scary to put yourself into a new, uncomfortable situation. The Bluefishing trick is to change your perception of what you're most afraid of. Are you afraid of growing? Of enjoying something new? Different? Or are you *more* afraid of feeling the same way you feel right now, stuck, on the same path, constantly knowing you're letting yourself down. Bluefishers are more afraid of *that*.

PUTTING ON THE RITZ

When I was much younger (just barely out of my bricklayer years), I was fascinated by these really, really expensive hotels. I thought to myself, "My God, these people must spend two thousand dollars a night just to sleep in those rooms. What the hell must it be like to be in that room?" I started going into the lobbies or the coffee shops of all these amazing hotels around me. In England, I'd go to the Ritz, sit in the lobby and just soak it in. I'd laugh to myself with excitement, "This is what it's like to be in the Ritz! I'm in the Ritz!" Then I'd walk out and guess what? I had been in the Ritz. I was now the kind of guy who went to the Ritz. So I went a step further. "Well, now, I wonder what the rooms are like." I went to the counter, polite as you please, and said, "I'll be back in town in two months and I'm booked at a hotel down the road, but I'm considering staying here instead. Could you show me one of your best rooms please?" Zero reason for them not to show me, so they did. Later, I left the hotel going, "I know what a two-thousand-dollar room looks like!" It was funny and I was having a giggle.

I didn't realize it at the time, but I was also breaking

down an internal boundary in my mind between what I had or what I was or what I did, and what I could have or what I could be or could do. I was soaking in the environment with all my senses, and it started to become more familiar to me.

Now, many years later, I've slept in a lot of hotels. But I've kept up my habit of exploring new ones. I've been in three times more hotels than I've stayed at, just to check them out, to see what they're like. If I have a trip to New York planned, before I go, I'll think to myself, "Which hotels haven't I been to? There's a new one here, and there's that one there." I'll phone ahead and say, "I'm traveling for business. I'm in the travel industry and I really want to know what's going on. I'm going to pop over to your hotel for a visit, is that okay?" Then, I'll head over and say, "Okay, show me your best room. Let's start top down. Show me your best room, then your middle room. I don't care about entry level. Not interested." I'll sample the best elements from different hotels. I do that a lot.

YOU DON'T HAVE TO OWN IT IN ORDER TO EXPERIENCE IT

It's not just that I care about doing a job of scoping out great places to impress my clients. It's also because, quite simply, if you want to know what it's like to drive a Ferrari, go to a Ferrari showroom and walk around, touch the cars, learn the history of that black-horse logo, ask questions of the salesperson. You don't need to have the money for it, the ownership of the thing, in order to have an experience. If you want to know what it's like to be in the best hotels, go and have a coffee in the lobby. This isn't about faking it; this isn't about trying to sound rich at dinner parties. This is about tasting something, just an element of it. A minute part of a bigger experience. And you know what? When you've tasted that, like the elastic band, you never go back. You can't unlearn that stuff, you can't unexperience it. Without ever blowing cash on the project, without faking anything at all, you now are the kind of person who knows about Ferraris and can recommend the best cappuccino at the Ritz.

So, now that you're a Bluefisher who is on a quest for new experiences and personal growth, you put yourself out there and you take it all in. You're in sponge mode. The sponge is one of the oldest organisms on the planet, and it hasn't changed, because it actually works. Unlike your bath sponge that gets full up with water, Bluefishing humans like us have an incredible ability to absorb and absorb and absorb and absorb. You have no limit. Sponge mode is a way to think of yourself so you can jump into the next thing knowing full well you can absorb any amount. You have no limit on how much you can absorb, experience, taste, feel, in essence, grow.

You can go bankrupt, you can lose your income, you can lose your business, but you can't lose experiences. You can't lose what you learn from experiencing situations with all of your senses.

SECRETS FROM
THE BLUEFISHING PLAYBOOK

* Enter Sponge Mode as often as possible. Walk in to a room to learn something new and say: "Hey, I'm an idiot right now, but I'm here to get just one percent smarter."

* If you stretch an elastic band five times, then let it go, it will never go back to the same small size it originally was. Same thing with you. Stretch yourself, and you'll never shrink back to where you started.

SEVENTEEN

LIVE WITH PASSION,
MOVE WITH PERSISTENCE

Honestly, I'm not sure I have much patience. I know it's a virtue, but too much of it, in my opinion, is no good.

When I want something to happen, when I'm passionate about it, I immediately need to know how we can create it. If I get myself into a dead end and see that there's a wall coming, I back up and go down a different path. Every single time. I have endless persistence in looking for a way to get to the goal. But the patience part is a tough one. My wife would laugh if she looked over my shoulder at this chapter. I have a low threshold for nonaction, because my passion harnesses my persistence and won't let a project or idea lay there like a couch potato.

If you can wrap *passion* and *persistence* together, you're invincible. It's the perfectly blended cocktail of champions. You can use it to scale walls, win fights, and instill belief, commitment, and passion in others. When I have to be *patient*, though, I can't. It's as simple as that. If I hit a brick wall, I don't wait and hope it will fall over, I don't wait for divine intervention, and I don't sit down and have a drink with my excuses. I find a way around it, over it, under it, or through it. As I've said, I come from a long line of brick masons. We can tear 'em down too.

THERE'S A THIN LINE BETWEEN PATIENCE AND COMPLACENCE

How patient should you be in business? Only as much as might generally be accepted as polite or reasonable. For example, how long would I wait for someone to return an important call that I made to them? I wait no longer than forty-eight hours. Period.

Patience can be a courtesy or a cop-out. I always advocate raw passion over patience because you won't need much waiting around if you have passion. Passion plus persistence will remove doors from their hinges, shred them, and throw them away.

It's not a coin toss. It's not a 50/50 proposition that you will succeed. When you go through something with passion and persistence together, you can't be blocked. You actually can't. It's not the case that you managed to get a foot in the door once but worry that the door can be shut again. *There's no longer a door.*

So, you've really got to live with passion and move with persistence. If you live any element of your life without passion, then you've got to ask the question, "Why are you doing that thing?" Now, you've got to pay the bills. We all have to do stuff that we don't enjoy. I have four dogs. Every day, I have to pick up their shit from the garden, and no way can I be excited about cleaning the crap off the lawn. This requirement of passion in our lives doesn't give you a loophole to be lazy. "Oh, sorry, not passionate about that task, I'm not going to do it."

THE GREATEST SALESMAN
I EVER KNEW

A long time back, I actually tried getting a job as an insurance agent. They sent me out with an old timer to get trained in the field. This was cold-call, knock-knock, door-to-door sales. This veteran fellow they put me with already had gotten his foot in the door at one house, so we both walked in to meet this nice couple, and my new colleague immediately says, "Let's talk over your debt scenario and your wills and your life insurance." He wasted no time putting his case forward. I kind of admired how direct he was.

He then turned around to the wife and said, "What would happen in the sad event that your husband didn't make it home tonight? He's dead. What are you doing tomorrow? Have you thought about it?"

And the husband said something and began to interrupt the insurance agent. The agent turned around and said, "Shut up. You're dead. You're not here. You can't get involved in this conversation."

Then he spoke to the wife again and the guy chimed in again. My man said, "You don't exist! You didn't make it home tonight, you don't have the chance to just pop over and go, 'Oh honey, I'm sorry. I died an hour ago but I left that policy I was supposed to sign in the top drawer of the credenza over there, underneath the magazines.' You don't have that ability."

The agent was charging so hard that he was rapidly alienating these people. You could see the guy didn't like this salesman, this smarmy insurance salesman doing this, and I felt how uncomfortable it was. The wife didn't know what to do and was trying to be polite. I squirmed and kept quiet.

But my guy was moving forward with persistence. He was going through this program which spelled out what insurance coverage they needed, exactly customized for them. He laid it out in front of the wife and said, "This is how much you need in order to look after you and little Johnny upstairs, and your house and the kids and their education. This is how much you need and this is what it's going to take to cover it, so that you won't have that horrible, uncomfortable feeling should it ever happen." He paused and then added, sincerely, "I hope this is a complete waste of money to you and that you never, ever need to use it. But if it's not, you know you're protected." And the wife and husband began to nod their heads in agreement.

I saw the wife give the husband a look, but he still seemed unsold. He was buying into the idea, but was not all the way ready. He said, "This is fantastic. Let us think about it."

My mentor (I had decided he was now, officially, my mentor) said, "Absolutely. No worry at all!" And he leaned back in his chair, puts his hand in his briefcase, pulled out a newspaper, crossed his leg over his other leg, and started reading the newspaper. I was sitting in an armchair next to him, and the couple were looking at me for answers and in my head I'm like, "I don't know what the fuck's going on here!" But I never said a word.

The husband finally said, "Excuse me." And my guy pulls down the corner of the paper, doesn't drop the whole news-paper. "Yeah?" Husband says, "We're gonna think about it and come back to you." "Yeah, I heard you," says my guy, and puts the paper back up again and starts reading it. The husband, obviously now a couple seconds away from getting pissed off, starts to say something and my guy just puts his newspaper down and says, "Look. I know you're going to have questions. Wouldn't they be best asked and answered while I'm here to help? So think of your questions, I'll read my newspaper, then you can ask all the questions you like."

They couple looked at each other and said, "I don't think we have any questions."

My mentor said, "Right! So, are we doing a ten-year policy or fifteen?"

The people signed.

And that was it. That was one of the most uncomfortable situations I've ever been in. I was a nineteen-year-old kid trying to get away from brickwork and I thought I was pretty tough, but that was the ballsiest thing I had ever seen. My guy went in and controlled the situation. He owned it. It was his. The husband and wife just didn't realize that they were bit players in his movie. Every time they tried to do something, he had such passion for his goal that he would say clearly, "I'm here so this situation doesn't happen! You've already been smart enough to let me come show you how this works. Don't be stupid and push me out, because the horrible situation we're talking about may be tomorrow." He was so strong, so full of conviction and force of will and belief that they bought into it.

I thought it was salesmanship. As we drove back to the office together, I thought, "Oh, this guy's made a commission, he's made loads of money, he was so cool. What a great salesman." But as he was driving, he was quiet, thinking. After a long period of silence, he turned to me and said, "Just imagine if tomorrow that man doesn't make it home. While it will be a devastating time, their finances will not be one of the reasons for them to be sad and confused."

I realized that, while he had made money from his work, he was actually motivated by a passion to do good for others. He believed in what he was selling. He truly didn't want those people to ever be in that situation.

Patience didn't help him sell. But passion and persistence combined did.

SECRETS FROM
THE BLUEFISHING PLAYBOOK

★ If you can wrap passion and persistence together, you're invincible.

★ There's a thin line between patience and complacence. Patience can be a cop-out.

EIGHTEEN

ACTUALLY GIVE A DAMN

I went to a Beverly Hills party the other night. It was a fundraiser for Hispanic women. Many of these types of events are good and have truly passionate people at them. But this one was unfortunately very artificial. It was not the event itself or the cause that was bad; it was the way most people just showed up to take pictures on the red carpet with the event's sign behind them, then left after the photo op. Those aren't supporters. That's not a community. That's not a pack.

If there were a top-five list of guidelines for my Blue-fishing business, the number-one thing on the list would be to have the relationship you want to have with your clients, colleagues, community, friends, and family. Then, things two through five would be to repeat the first one.

That is how powerful it is to me; everything else is completely out the window.

It goes back to the six-year-old on the playground who only played with the kids he wanted to play with. Sure, I want clients. I want customers. But I want relationships more.

There was a time in the early years of Bluefish where things were going well but I wasn't taking the business too seriously. You'd think I'd have at least taken it financially seriously, but I didn't pay much attention to that part yet either. I only wanted to spend time with people I liked. I only wanted to phone people that I liked. I didn't accept many people into my circle. Had I realized that I was making money from doing exactly this, I think I would have diluted myself, I would have started letting more people in, and I'd have killed the brand and what it stood for. Instead, I thought: "The stakes are not that high, this is just a little gig. I am not going to dilute what I want for any reason." That's where the power of stupidity, maybe ignorance, maybe stubbornness, can be a good thing.

The lesson here is to take money out of the equation, if you can. Money drives our emotional and physical states, but when you can take money out of the equation, you become a lot more based on principle. When I was starting to build this dream, I knew that my end goal was to have a bunch of people around that I liked, that I could then go get a real job with. This was my own career community that I was building up. This was my very own personalized Monster.com.

FOCUS ON THE RELATIONSHIP

The only thing I do today is manage and maintain relationships. I have relationships with vendors. I have relationships with attorneys, with agents, with management firms, with celebrities, with clients, with suppliers, with hotels. I have different relationships with different people. Everything else is just conversation in the right place at the right time. All those other things just fall into place.

I try to look for those people that carry the same kind of thoughts as me, the same kind of values and morals as me. And then the big question comes in again: "Can I have a relationship with this person?"

You'd be amazed at how many arrogant pricks there are who say to me, 'Hey, I want to go to this party because George Lucas is there, or I want to show Demi Moore my script. Can you make that happen?" Of course I can, but my answer is no. My ethos is: Do I like you? Can I deal with you? Are you real? Or have you got your head up your ass?

It's the exact same for my team as it is for my clients. I don't have business cards and half my team doesn't either. We don't even have titles. There's no VP, president, none of that because we're in a relationship and we bring people into the relationship that are required to help the other person's relationship.

There's nothing original about what we do at Bluefish. This is where it comes down to, I suppose, the stupidity and the ugly, as I have described them throughout this book. This is nothing new. There is no change in the shape of a wheel here. It's a simple six-year-old's gut reaction to play with those he wants to play with. Just a bunch of people doing good work with people they like. That's always been the dream.

ACTUALLY GIVE A DAMN

It's so important to be yourself with your customers, clients, and colleagues. If you're genuine, if you treat them as you want to be treated, with their best interests in mind, that changes the nature of your relationship.

That's why I do my homework every time. I research what people like so that I know what means a lot to them. They want to go into space, they want to dive to the bottom of the ocean, they like Bentleys, they like Maroon 5—

doesn't matter. There could be chocolates, a signed guitar, tickets to a baseball game, a free Jaguar test drive on a race-course. Could be a donation to Autism Speaks, could be reservations for that little Thai place only you know about in Bangkok because you happen to know they love Panang Curry as much as you do. It's finding something custom-ized to them that you can surface and give to them and say sincerely: "I did this just for you. Not for anyone else. You."

LISTEN AND ACT

The trick here is to get creative and resourceful. Think about the person you want to do something special for. Do they have kids? Ask about them. Do they have pets? I have a Shih Tzu; that leads to all kinds of conversations. Do they like music? They could wind up meeting Bocelli or jamming with Billy Gibbons, the guitarist for ZZ Top. So, listen to their voice, find where it starts to get faster and more natural, look for whatever dead giveaway they have and follow the trail. Then you'll know where there could be an opportunity for a nice personal touch, be-cause you care, you actually care enough about this person and relationship to seriously think about what could mean a lot to this person. That would show that you took the time to listen and to act—those two things together are a powerful combo. It's never, not once, never going to be enough to go, "Oh, well, if I can ever do anything for you someday. . . ."

SOMEDAY DOESN'T MEAN ANYTHING

Someday doesn't mean anything. Today matters. You have to make it mean something. Be present, be there for them. I only take on clients I like so that when I do something that shows I give a shit about them: I actually do. I'm a lousy pretender.

Any successful client relationship boils down to listening. (This applies to every relationship, for that matter). A lot of people miss that. You can't dominate the conversation; you have to let that go. I say, "Play it where it lands." And you never know where it's going to land, so be open. You can't be open if you're not fully aware and engaged in that moment. You know when you're talking to someone and they start browsing around on their iPhone? Or when you're on a call and you hear them typing out emails in the background? That's when I'm done. They don't care enough about this relationship for me to give it my time.

The ones you have to watch out for are the people who pretend to be perfect. If you're on one side of the equal sign and they're on the other, and they're perfect, then what do you think they want from you? An equal amount of fake bullshit. They're chasing something that doesn't exist. That's not someone you want to deal with.

MANAGE EXPECTATIONS (SO THAT YOU CAN TRULY OVERDELIVER)

Here's something I had to learn to do well the hard way in relationships: manage expectations. "Yeah, yeah," you're saying, "there's nothing new here," but this is so important, it's worth seeing an example about going about it Bluefish-style.

A client calls me up and asks about something he wants to do, and I say, "I think we can arrange something like that for you." Say they want to meet Tiger Woods. Let's say I know Tiger has a charity for kids, I'm making this part up, fill in whatever blanks. I love working with charities, I'm always happy to help them out, I've got my BLUEcause organization—it's some of the most important work in the world. So, for this story, I'm happy to work it out so that my client can donate to Tiger's organization. If Tiger's happy to drive a couple of balls with my guy, that's great. If it leads to more, that's great too. Here's the important part. I don't tell my client what's up. I play where it lands. He thinks he's going to get an autograph at most. But my team and I have been working behind the scenes, we sneaked his clubs out onto the green, our guy gets to meet Tiger, and Tiger might ask him to hit a couple balls, could turn into eighteen. Things like this happen all the time, and when it does and you see the guy, he's over the moon and it's a day he'll remember forever.

That's not a win-win. It's *exponential wins*. Money moves and flows, but Bluefishing's about so much more than that. Like barter in the old days, before money. I get this, you get that, and we're both happy, plus a whole lot more. Nobody uses anybody, nobody feels used, and way beyond that, everybody feels good about what they're doing. What you're dealing with here is not money. It's people. Money's a symbol. It's the people who use the symbols.

CLEAR YOUR HEAD ENOUGH TO HEAR IT

That to me is what life's really about: my people. I don't want to go to my deathbed with any regrets. Regrets are hard to avoid altogether, but I think if they don't weigh nearly as much as the good things you did for good people, that's a good life.

The real question is, how do you know what to do now, so you wind up in a good place later? Here's the trick:

Your gut tells you. Clear your head enough to hear it—like I said, hit the punching bag, go out for a run, play some Mahjong, whatever helps you purge your stress and anxiety and replace it with a simple, momentary state of openness and focus.

If you still need help, try this technique. It's a big one. I did this one time and it got me thinking so much I couldn't sleep. But I couldn't forget it either, so I started doing it more, and once in a while it's a helpful tool for getting your brain organized. Here's what I do: I lie in bed and I imagine it's my deathbed. Grim, I know! But hear me out. Here's what I'm thinking, "Sims, you've got unfinished business. You have people to see through stuff. You have a beautiful wife and things you want to make happen together. You have to get all the kids through school, raised right, college if they want, they might have kids, and man, you want to see that." You know what happens to you? Probably a little bit of panic if your life has gone off the rails and you know in your gut that you're not doing your best work. But the upside of this exercise is that you get laser focus!

Since I'm in the business of delivering ultimate life experiences for my clients, I use this technique in my work too. I constantly ask myself what would my clients look back on in life that would mean the most to them? That's how you create unique, big, *personal* experiences for people. You give to *them* specifically. Not a one-size-fits-all thing they can get anywhere. Everybody else does that. That's just called shopping. This is called Bluefishing.

SECRETS FROM
THE BLUEFISHING PLAYBOOK

* Have the relationship you want to have. If there were a Top Five list of guidelines for Bluefishing, the number-one thing on the list would be to have the relationship you want to have with your clients, colleagues, community, friends, and family. Then things two through five would be to repeat the first one.

* Take money out of the equation (if you can). Money drives our emotional and physical states, but when you can take money out of the equation, you get to act based on principle.

* When you do something or give something, make sure you can honestly say: "I did this just for you. Not for anyone else. You."

* Someday doesn't mean anything. Never plan for someday. Today is what matters.

NINETEEN

DON'T COUNT
YOUR LOSSES

I mentioned my early job of selling life insurance when I was nineteen. It was one of those gigs that only later in life did I realize taught me a lot about forming positive mental work habits. Like many of my other so-called careers, my insurance gig was a very short one. One of the things I had to do was cold call on the phone. I had to be the annoying little shit that phoned you right when you were sitting down to dinner with your family. "Hey, Mr. Whatever, I want to talk to you about what happens to your family in the case of your death." I was that guy.

It was a horrible job. But not for the reason that most people hate cold calling; I didn't have phone phobia. It wasn't the fact that I was working in the evening. I'd work through to one o'clock in the morning or work twenty-four hours straight; late work and hard hours never bothered me. I also didn't have a problem with the smile and dial aspect. Taking a note from my mentor that I told you a story about earlier, I too honestly believed that I was helping the people I called gain security, protection, and support in their old age. When I called these people up, I truly believed I was doing them a service.

My problem was with the list. They gave us a big list, like a book, every Monday when you showed up at work. They were nothing more than glorified, mass-bound phone books. You'd go through each one, phone number by phone number, working your way through, and dive into your spiel: "Hello Mr. or Mrs. X, how ya doing? I'm glad I caught you." Whatever their response was, you had to mark it exactly on a spreadsheet. This spreadsheet included what time you dialed, what the outcome was, is an appointment set yes or no. Doing that kind of paperwork doesn't bother me either. I believe there's a certain accountability in it. But if you think about the amount of successes or wins you get in that line of procedural cold-calling work, the percentage is not high. I remember it to now when I'm doing my business and working on different projects with different clients. All the no's in the world are what make the yesses feel like magic.

STOP COUNTING YOUR LOSSES

Here's what pissed me off about the list. What we were all really doing on that insurance spreadsheet was recording our losses. Notice that I didn't use the word *failure*. I'm a great believer in failure, as you know. These were distinct losses. These were things that *I lost*. I lost the opportunity to speak to these people, to bring them something of value. The bosses wanted us to record all the bad things that were said. I had to write down the exact response, word for word, such as, "Go get a real job," or "Screw off." Happy stuff like that, followed by a slammed phone.

Think about your own week. How many times does something go miraculously, shockingly, brilliantly right? Maybe a few times? I celebrate those now, big time. Everybody should. It's so easy to take a little win and pat yourself on the back for being productive and move on, because you're already on to the next thing. But taking a moment to put some thought, some feeling, into the little accomplishments—that's motivating.

What if every one of your losses every day was recorded in front of you? Every one of your losses would be there to greet you again the next day. In that cold-calling job, that was the norm. I'd come in to work, fresh new day, lots of motivation. I'd get to my desk, got my cup of tea, got my sweets, get ready for my smile and dial, open up the book, get the call sheet out, and BANG! There they were. All the times I was told to "go eff yourself!" or "Why are you interrupting our dinner?" All this negativity. And it was being recorded!

Coming in to look at how many *losses* I had and face all that negativity from the night before, that was severely depressing for me. Worse, it was utterly nonmotivational. Antimotivational. "Last night was a waste of your existence. Hey, have a good night tonight!" I couldn't handle it.

So, simple as you please, I started to just flip the sheet over. Now, I'm looking at a blank piece of paper instead of my losses. As I call people, I doodle smiley faces, happy faces, sad faces, horns on their heads, a doodle to describe each response. I draw a little face, and there's steam coming out of its ears. This guy's furious. I'm messing around with my drawings, sure, but I am also reporting on the calls in my own way. A way that'll make it humorous to me, instead of bleak.

I did my doodle reporting for about a week, then I was called into the office. My boss had my scribble sheets. On the front where I'm supposed to fill in all this information, blank. Nothing. On the back, pictures of motorbikes and hamburgers with smiley faces and whatever I wanted to bloody do while people were telling me to "Never call this number again!" On the other side, I would record my appointments, I'd make a little note, put a little star, big fat smiley face, not in the proper box, just on the page itself. I didn't record the go fuck yourselves. I found I was more positive, and I could manage my way through many more phone calls and I started to take pleasure and pride in those small wins, when I had a chance to draw a big star on the page.

And what do you think happened? The boss fired me.

I didn't care. I had learned something! This was my first experience with consciously building new habits. Sometimes you have to flip the page over and start a new cycle, one that's focused on something positive.

Habits are good when they are paired up with accountability. Here's why. When you've got passion, you've got fuel. It's an accelerator, and that speeding train can ride off the rails if you don't get people around you to support you and hold you accountable to keep everything clean and moving in the right direction. Sometimes, you find that you're going along at top speed, because that's the way we are, we're entrepreneurs, we jump in and go full on, and then you realize you're almost out of tracks. "Shit, I haven't got the right infrastructure." You have to create it as you move. You have to know that when someone says they're going to do something, it's done *yesterday*. If you can pair up passion with a habit for accountability, and instill that in all the people you work with, you will quite literally keep yourself on track.

The Bluefishing entrepreneur also has to stay agile, flexible, and constantly willing to adapt and change. You need to get away from too many rigid rituals, habits, or ways of thinking. The only habit should be that you're damn good at what you do. Your habit should be to recognize success. Don't recognize losses. That will demotivate you, it will get you low, and the lower you get the further you have to go to get up. Negativity is the opposite of passion. It is the silent assassin that kills most people's motivation.

BEWARE THE LUCKY SOCKS

That said, I also think habits should not be turned into rituals. Rituals can too easily become superstitions: crutches and excuses that are actually based on fear. Many people seem to love to have something they can lean on to say, "Ah, this didn't work, because I didn't have my good socks on!" That's a rancid habit, you know? Or they get to ten o'clock in the morning, and something has gone wrong already, and they say, "I'm having the worst day, this day sucks." But it's only ten o'clock in the morning! If you ever do that, stop. Just stop yourself right where you are. Flip the page over and stop counting your losses.

You've heard of baseball players who won't cut their hair or they wear dirty socks, weird pendants and such. You've seen *Major League*. Aren't people with these superstitions just setting themselves up to fail? What if someone steals their lucky charm? I've never understood giving an object the power over whether I win or lose. Why would I put my success, ability, credibility, career, livelihood, life, all on the line for the color of my socks? It's always boggled me.

The one way I can see this working out in your favor is if the thing is helping you get motivated. There is a zone. You've been there. You know, where you get into that place where the passion, commitment, ability, they all come together. You're in it, and you're at the top of your game. Whatever helps you get there, hey, I'm with you.

There are tools you can use to help you get into your zone. It may be doing jumping jacks. Say you do a warm-up before a public speaking event. Tony Robbins hops on his trampoline before going on stage. There's the person who warms up her vocal cords before she sings. This is preparation, this is warm-up, this is a trigger to get into your zone. This is very different from wearing your favorite cap backward and hoping you get lucky. You are far greater than the color of your socks.

ROW ALL DAY LONG

A guy who works for me has a hand-carved model Viking ship that his daughter brought him from Norway. It's right there on his desk and he sees it every day when he sits down. He told me he looks at it and is reminded, "Man, I can row all day long, just like my ancestors did." That's a motivational thing. It's a tool to say don't give up. That's getting yourself in the zone, psyching yourself up. These are tools of the trade. They're not crutches.

I think your physical space is really important too. Where do you work? Where do you think best? What's an environment that helps you get in the zone? You can't always be there, but knowing your terrain is always smart. I'm a great believer in the mancave or womancave. You know what that cave represents? Your time.

BE AS SELFISH AS YOU HAVE TO BE

I'm a great believer in being selfish. You absolutely have to be, at various times in your day, relentlessly selfish in order to focus on you and your work, because that's what keeps the whole ship sailing. That's what puts food on the table. In this case, I'm defining selfish as being totally in tune with your own self. You have to allow yourself rest and recreation. If you do that, then you can give more of yourself to those closest to you.

My mancave happens to be my garage, and it's my escape zone. The world is going so fast, it's constantly evolving at such an exponential rate. Every day something is different from yesterday. Every day something is revealed that we can use, whether it be an app, an attitude, or a new series you have to follow. There's always something. Nothing stays still anymore from day to day, and I love this motion and growth. But in order to recognize it, there are those moments you have to stand still. You've just got to eject. Out of all of it. Clear your head. Reset. Recalibrate. Figure out how to tune in to yourself, or you can't hear your own thoughts for all the noise.

So many people have talked to me about the wonders of meditation. For me, I can't do it sitting still. If I plunk down to meditate, I go, "Shit! I never responded to that email, or, Oh my God, Sims, what are you doing sitting there on your ass, you should be doing ninety-nine other things . . ." My meditation is different. It's in riding a motorcycle or getting into the boxing ring. It's that moment when you focus so much on something that everything else in your day and work and life falls away. A lot of stand-up comics have talked about this. When they get up on stage to perform, they are so focused on their craft and so in the moment doing something they love, that all the rest of the day disappears. That's a form of release for them.

The beautiful thing about life is that there are so many ways to release your mind. It can be through yoga, meditation, or extreme sports, anything that takes you away from whatever routine or problem is bogging you down. Afterward, when you step back into the world, sure, all the worries settle back in to sit on your shoulders, but now you're realigned and perfectly ready to handle them.

That's why I'm a great believer in being selfish, in rewarding yourself for your victories, focusing on yourself, and getting out of your own way. We're very, very good about recharging our daily stuff. We remember to plug in our phones, charge the car, or put gas into it. The only thing you don't recharge is yourself.

YOUR RIGHT TO RECHARGE

You have to realize that and use your right to say, "Yes, there's a lot going on at the moment, and a lot of people need things from me, but you know, I need to be the best person I can, so I'm taking half an hour to go run." I get seriously funny, disapproving looks on the day when shit's hitting the fan, and everything's going wrong, and I say:

"I'm gonna ride my bike around the canyons." Or "I'm gonna be over here reading a book for thirty minutes," or "I'm gonna go to the gym now." They're like, "Steve, we need to get this done today!" I don't let it ruffle me, I stay calm and say, "We will. But first, I'm going to take half an hour to do this." Without realizing it, you're recharging.

I think it's the important thing to do, especially in this entrepreneurial world where we are literally creating products and jobs and the future from scratch. The more passionate we are about something, the more we have to set aside time to recharge, retune, reset. We must. In fact, it's one of the first things I tell people. You want to hold onto this speeding train? That's great, but every now and then, you've got to get off, let a few trains pass you by, so that you can pick your next train and jump on for the ride of your life.

What we're really talking about is getting to euphoria, nirvana, that inner utopia. That happens the moment when you're in your zone. It's that place where you just kind of separate from reality, float away from normal space/time. That's when you know you're doing something worthwhile, that's when you're a Bluefishing master.

Here's something that always amazes me at the boxing gym. You walk in and hear punching and grunting all around the gym. Everyone's working out hard, so you hear them slapping on the bags. It's noisy. Then you get in the ring with a guy, and he's coming at you, and all of a sudden, everything goes quiet. You can't hear the bags, you can't hear shouting, all you hear is the bum-bum, bum-bum, bum-bum, your heart. You're in that place. The zone. That's what I strive for. That's the utopia that we're looking for. It's a reprieve. Not only is it a reward for your work, it recharges you, and gives you access to depths you didn't imagine.

SECRETS FROM
THE BLUEFISHING PLAYBOOK

★ Consciously build new habits. Day start off on the wrong foot? Here's a trick. Write down your 'losses' for the morning on a piece of paper. Then flip the paper over and start fresh. Write down your small wins on that side. Learn to celebrate tiny successes, and put the losses behind you.

★ Negativity is the opposite of passion. It is the silent assassin that kills most people's motivation.

★ Be as selfish as you have to be. You have a right to recharge yourself. Take it and defend it.

TWENTY

THE BLUEFISHING
PLAYBOOK

When people say "the stars are aligned," or "your ducks are in a row"—you know it's not luck, right? It's you.

I can't stand this idea of luck. That you're lucky to get that girl, you're lucky to have such a successful career, or when someone says, "You know, it's funny. The harder I work, the luckier I get."

Nope, not luck. What is happening in that moment is this: Everything you've been doing, all the hard work that has gone on, beneath the surface, the emotional digging for authenticity, all your efforts to observe and absorb and change and grow and evolve and succeed, all that suddenly leads to a moment when you're on top of it all.

STACK YOUR DECK

Bluefishing is a mentality first, and then it's a stack of tools and behaviors that add up to incredible achievements. You start by looking at yourself and running an audit on your life. Then you dig deep into your passion, finding out what it is and listening for it in others. Then you apply perseverance, and layer on a whole lot of real deal authenticity for your own personal brand and all your relationships. At that point, all that's left is to stay on top of your game by practicing saying no, orchestrating talent around you, and remembering to constantly soak in 1 percent more experience and, yes, failure, than you knew yesterday.

What I've laid out in this book is a series of stories, beliefs, and tools for living the life you want to live and getting anything done. It's a book of building blocks, and once you've learned them, you can climb them to the very top of the world. And that, *that* is Bluefishing. You want to know how you knock down walls? You don't even see them anymore, because you're so far above them.

You've got it in you, Bluefisher, but if you ever lose your way, just come back to this Playbook, say the password, and the door will open and you're on your way.

One fish, two fish, red fish . . .

THE BLUEFISHING PLAYBOOK

1. Throw away the "That could never be me" mentality. Instead, ask, "Why couldn't it?"

2. No one ever drowned from falling in the water. They drowned from staying there. Don't be afraid to jump, Bluefisher. Be afraid of standing still.

3. Avoid Analysis Paralysis. While other people are planning things to an early death, Bluefishers have already tried something 4 Different Ways And Learned What Works.

4. There's a password for every door. You just have to listen for it.

5. Don't be easy to understand, be impossible to *mis*understand.

6. Nothing's ever going to happen if it benefits only you. Work for win-win, every time.

7. Ask Why at Least Three Times: The first why is what they think they think, the second why is what they think you want to hear, the third why is what they feel.

8. The experience beats the cash, every time. Cash gets spent and forgotten. An experience you can give to someone sticks forever.

9. Passion Is Something You Have to Discover. Relax. Try stuff. It takes time. But never stop looking.

10. If you knew that the Earth was going to collide with Mars tomorrow, what would you do right now? Maybe that's your passion.

11. Do Not Believe What People Tell You. Most don't have the ability to communicate effectively. All of their best information is unsaid, somewhere between the lines. Drill down for it.

12. Actually Give a Damn. If *You* don't believe in it, *They* won't believe in it.

13. Failure is just an education in what not to do. For every failure, you're learning. Take pride in your scars.

14. What people think about you is just their perception, it's not a fact about you.

15. What happens to you is not your obituary. Get back up again, Bluefisher.

16. It's not about your IQ. It's about your I Can.

17. A handwritten note beats an email every single time: It takes less than a second to delete an email,

but a minimum of three minutes (and a lot more emotion) to discard something real.

18. Let people know you're thinking about them. It goes far.

19. "Ugly" works. For Bluefishers, ugly means raw, unpolished, quick, and real. It's the opposite of overpolished, CGI and corporate.

20. Do a self-audit, because things don't magically get better. Take an honest look at your strengths and weaknesses. Invest in the strengths and see what weaknesses you need to remove.

21. How Do You Walk into a Room? Personal branding is not marketing and Twitter followers. It's figuring out your core persona. Who you are, not who they want you to be.

22. Don't waste your time counting likes: You'll never be able to pay your bar tab with Facebook likes. . . .

23. Try the Chug Test. If you want to know if someone is a good match for you (as a client, customer, vendor, boss, employee, friend), ask yourself: Would I chug a beer with that person?

24. Master the courage to say no: Remember the more you bring into your life, the more you dilute what you can do well.

25. Audit Your Inner Circle: *No* gives you the ability to fire the vampires. You can fire customers. You can even fire friends. Determine who adds energy to your time and who sucks it out.

26. There's a difference between being able to do everything and *doing* everything.

27. You can only grow by giving other people responsibility. That's the only way you and your business will ever manage to scale.

28. It's About Time: The real art of delegation, Bluefish style, is actually about learning how to put time into what matters. This means learning how not to spend time on things that slow you down.

29. "Great" is not a goal you can see. If you want to make your business great, first work to make it better than it was yesterday.

30. Get the right people to say the right things about you. That's marketing in a nutshell.

31. You can't concentrate on your friends when you're giving all your time to strangers.

32. Don't let technology set the rules for your communication. If you hide behind emails and tweets, no one will ever hear you.

33. If communication isn't personal, it's not communication.

34. Have someone with credibility at a party telling five people that you're the magical gold dust they need. That's better marketing than sending out twenty-thousand emails.

35. Enter Sponge Mode as often as possible. Walk in to a room to learn something new and say: "Hey, I'm an idiot right now, but I'm here to get just one percent smarter."

36. If you stretch an elastic band five times, then let it go, it will never go back to the same small size it originally was. Same thing with you. Stretch yourself, Bluefisher, and you'll never shrink back to where you started.

37. If you can wrap passion and persistence together, you're invincible.

38. There's a thin line between patience and complacence. Patience can be a cop-out.

39. Have the relationship you want to have. If there were a Top Five List of guidelines for Bluefishing, the number one thing on the list would be to have the relationship you want to have with your clients, colleagues, community, friends, and

family. Then things two through five would be to repeat the first one.

40. Take money out of the equation (if you can). Money drives our emotional and physical states, but when you can take money out of the equation, you get to act based on principle.

41. When you do something or give something, make sure you can honestly say: "I did this just for you. Not for anyone else. You."

42. Someday doesn't mean anything. Never plan for someday. Today is what matters.

43. Consciously build new habits. Day start off on the wrong foot? Here's a trick. Write down your so-called losses for the morning on a piece of paper. Then flip the paper over and start fresh. Write down your small wins on that side. Learn to celebrate tiny successes, and put the losses behind you.

44. Negativity is the opposite of passion. It is the silent assassin that kills most people's motivation.

45. Be as selfish as you have to be. You have a right to recharge yourself. Take it and defend it. That's the only way you'll be able to harness your own energy to make things happen.

There you go. That's the secret playbook. Unlocked and there for the taking. The deck is stacked in your favor.

I hope you'll use these tools to open all the doors in your life and make real magic happen.

And when it works for you, drop me a note, master Bluefisher.

—*Steve Sims*

APPENDIX: LIVE A LITTLE

BLUEFISH EXPERIENCES

At Bluefish, my company, we don't talk a lot about the amazing things we pull off for our clients. Those are experiences customized just for them, not for anyone else. But, from time to time, it's okay to share some of our stories. By way of showing you some of the "totally out of reach" things I have been able to make happen by using the Bluefishing tools in this book, you might just be inspired to do some of your own!

I hope you enjoy this fun list of things we've made happen.

OUT OF THIS WORLD EXPERIENCES

* Submarine trip to the *Titanic*
* Be James Bond for a weekend
* Hang out or jam out with a celebrity recording artist

- ★ Private cooking lessons with LA's finest executive chefs
- ★ Go on a luxury safari in the Amazon and Serengeti
- ★ Partake in a filmed marine conservation expedition in the Pacific Islands
- ★ Play drums with Guns & Roses drummer Matt Sorum
- ★ Play guitar with ZZ Top's Billy Gibbons
- ★ Sardine Run
- ★ Sing on stage with Journey
- ★ Have Florida Georgia Line sing Happy Birthday to you backstage
- ★ Meet and Greet with your favorite recording artist or celebrity
- ★ Appear as a walk-on role on your favorite TV show

ADRENALINE EXPERIENCES

- ★ Fly an L-39 in an edge of space flight
- ★ Drive a supercar 200 miles per hour
- ★ Swim with the sharks in South Africa
- ★ Train with Navy Seals

* Drive a Formula 1 car

* Stunt driving experiences

* Halo Jump

* Heli-skiing in Switzerland

* Hot air balloon ride over Tanzania

* Take the Top Gun challenge and fly a military jet

* Train with Special Ops

* Private race car lessons with a top race icon

* Laser dog fight in L39's over the Mojave

* Drive a Lotus F1 car and ride passenger with
  Randay Mamola on a Ducati GP bike

SPORTING EXPERIENCES

* Watch Formula 1 in Monaco with royalty

* Private golf lessons with an iconic Green Jacket

* Paddock Club Access to all Formula 1 races

* Attend the Kentucky Derby in Millionaire's Row

* Private polo lessons with a top polo player

* Olympic Bobsleigh Run

* VIP Party access at the Super Bowl

* Sit courtside at a basketball game

* Watch a soccer game with the chairman of a
  British football team in his boxclub 2

EXCLUSIVE EXPERIENCES

* Arranged a private dinner for 6 at the feet of Michelangelo's David while being sung to by Andrea Bocelli

* Backstage and front row seats to New York, Paris, London, LA and Milan Fashion Week

* Front row at Victoria Secret Fashion Show and Pink carpet access to the after party

* Sourced 16 Birkin handbags in 2 weeks

* VIP/Red Carpet Access at the World's Top Award Shows and Movie Premieres

* Perks and Upgrades at the World's Top 5 Star Hotels & Resorts

* Access to Playboy Mansion parties

* Exotic car purchases (For example, a 1960's Ferrari)

* Retain a private island for up to 200 guests

* Book castles for intimate stays, family vacations, and corporate events

* A last-minute private charter plane and a guide for the day to visit the Iguassu Falls in Brazil

* Fort Denison in Sydney Harbor for a private function on NYE to enjoy unobstructed views of the fireworks

- ★ A crime tour in London with a crime expert and a tour of Stonehenge and Bath with an Oxford Professor
- ★ A private Hollywood movie screening for 150 people before it's released to the public
- ★ Private dinner/lunch with captains of industry that included the Trump family and Mark Burnett
- ★ Play with rockets at the Mojave space port
- ★ Backstage at a Broadway show
- ★ VIP day at Miami Art Basel events
- ★ New XBox and PlayStations before release dates

ACKNOWLEDGMENTS

I've been interviewed a lot over the last twenty years. I've been on television, I've been featured in magazines, I've been in the news. But Jayson Gaignard was the first person to ask me to get up on stage *not* to talk about the world of luxury, but to talk about ME—about my experiences and ideas about life and business. I'm really glad he asked.

Then, suddenly, people started saying, "Sims, you should write a book." Then Tucker Max (thanks, Tucker) told me to actually go write the damn thing. Thanks to Philip McKernan for further sealing my fate by telling me I had a *duty* to write the book, to my agents Scott Hoffman and Frank Weimann at Folio for making sure I did, and, of course, to Michele Martin at North Star and Simon & Schuster for making sure the world had the opportunity to read it.

I have been blessed to meet amazing people from all walks of life, and I believe I am a combination of all them, as I've learned something critical from each one, especially

Joe Polish, Dean Jackson, Colin West, Greg Reid, Peter Diamandis, and Jay Abraham. That's an incomplete list, of course, as those are just a few of the amazing people I'm honored and blessed to be able to call friends.

To all the people over the years who took a chance on me, and who risked believing in what I did, who I am, and how I live: Without you, there would be no stories to put in the book in the first place.

To all those who taught me how to fight (and when not to): Thank you.

And of course, to my amazing family and loves of my life, Clare, Henry, Lily, and George: You all made me want to be better than I was. You make me want to be better still, every day. Thank you.

ABOUT THE AUTHOR

Steve Sims has been running his luxury travel and lifestyle concierge firm, Bluefish, for more than twenty years. With his unique talent for connecting with people's passions, opening doors, and making things happen, Sims has developed an exclusive reputation and impressive client list of the world's rich and famous. Bluefish has offices around the world and has been featured in *Forbes*, the *New York Times*, *Entrepreneur*, *Variety*, *Worth*, CNBC, and many other media outlets. Sims is also a keynote speaker at venues including Harvard and the Pentagon, and has spoken at many top entrepreneurial groups, including Mastermind Talks, Genius Networking Events, and Entrepreneur Society of SF. He lives in Los Angeles with his wife, kids, dogs, and a lot of motorcycles.